Youth A Part

Young People and the Church

)

D

The vision is for a Church which takes young people seriously. It is a Church where young people fully and actively participate at every level. It is a Church which is built on good relationships, where young people particularly are concerned, not only with each other, but with those inside and outside the Church. It is a Church where there is a good theological understanding of why and how it goes about its work with young people. It is a Church which recognises that work of this quality needs resources and has the faith and courage to commit significant resources to the young people in the Church.

Youth A Part (*paragraph* 9.1)

ERRATUM
In paragraph 1 on page 95 of *Youth A Part*, the total number of people baptised should read 174,125 not 956,125. Thus the number of young people baptised between the ages of 10 and 25 represent 3% of this total, not 0.5%.

Youth A Part

Young People and the Church

National Society / Church House Publishing
Church House, Great Smith Street, London SW1P 3NZ

ISBN 0 7151 4864 8

GS 1203

Published 1996 for the General Synod Board of Education jointly by the National Society and Church House Publishing, with funding from the Department for Education

Second impression 1996

Acknowledgements

All the statistics, except those otherwise acknowledged, have been provided by The Young People and the Church Today Project based at the Centre for Theology and Education, Trinity College, Carmarthen. Project Directors: Reverend Leslie Francis and David Lankshear; Research Officers: Clare Williamson and Mandy Robins.

The working party appreciate and thank all of those who have contributed to the research, particularly, Jeff Astley, Tim Clapton, John Richardson and Daniel Tyndall who allowed unpublished material to be used for the report. Also Sheila Lev, Valerie Anderson and Lindsay Echlin who provided excellent administrative support.

This report has only the authority of the Board by which it was prepared

Cover design by Leigh Hurlock

Printed in England by The Cromwell Press, Melksham, Wiltshire

Contents

Foreword by the Archbishop of Canterbury   vii

Members of the Working Party   xi

Working Party Terms of Reference   xii

Introduction   1

1.   Youth Cultures and Christian Cultures   6
    Issues that are important to young people   6
    Challenging the Church   10
    Young People in a 'post-modern' world   11
    The 'gap' between youth cultures and church cultures   12
    Young people's attendance at church   13
    Church and Christian cultures   14
    Young people's access to Church   16
    Working in different contexts   17
    Conclusion   22

2.   A Theology for Youth Work   23
    Youth work and the mission of God   23
    Youth work is mission in the context of culture   25
    Youth work is culture-forming   28
    Youth work is concerned with personal development   32
    Youth work is incarnational   34
    Youth work is relational   36
    Youth work is a call to discipleship   36
    Youth work is community building   37
    Conclusion   38

3.   Working Spiritually   39
    Within the community   45
    Education   55
    Personal journeys   60

4.   Young People's Space   63
    Worship   63
    Young people in the structures of the Church   72

	Taking young people seriously	76
	Conclusion	79
5.	Working with Relationships	80
	Building relationships	80
	Outreach work – new initiatives to young people outside the Church	86
	Working relationships in small groups	91
	Baptism, confirmation and marriage	94
	Conclusion	98
6.	Working with Those who Work with Young People	100
	Volunteers in youth work	104
	Employing a paid youth worker	109
	Resources	118
	Good practice in youth work	121
	Clergy involvement in youth work	125
	Conclusion	126
7.	Working in Partnership	127
	Partnership networks	127
	Working with local authorities	130
	Working with uniformed organisations	138
	Working with other agencies and networks	142
	Ecumenical work	145
	Interfaith work	145
	Conclusion	147
8.	The Church's Role – Past, Present and Future	148
	Perspectives from past work	148
	Future trends	158
	Conclusion	160
9.	Recommendations and Objectives	161
	Appendix: Types of Youth Work	188
	Bibliography	191
	Index	194

Foreword by
the Archbishop of Canterbury

Like many others my late teens and early twenties were crucial in the formation of my Christian faith. It was when I was seventeen that my brother, Bob, first invited me along to our local Church which he had started going to some years before. There I, in my turn, moved from a reverent agnosticism into a living faith. That change is not something I can put a date to, but some time early in 1953 it gradually happened.

The years that followed were equally momentous. My time in the Youth Group gave me the grounding in the Bible Study, Church membership, worship and private prayer which have stood me in good stead ever since. But it was as much what the youth leaders did as what they said that really impressed me. Here were people who were prepared to take time with me – who believed that who I was, and the questions I had, really mattered. The debt I owe to the likes of Ron Rushmer, Eileen Hood, Terry Nottage and other young people, to say nothing of discerning, caring clergy is incalculable.

National Service followed and it was in Iraq that I first began to think that God might be calling me into the Ordained Ministry. Stuck out in the desert, without a chaplain in sight, I, and one or two others, took it in turns to lead services and to speak at them. That first taste of Christian ministry was something that excited me and kept me enthusiastic in the years that followed.

Reading *Youth A Part* has reminded me vividly of those years in my own life. More than that, it underlines time and again the importance to our health as a Church in having a strong work with and among young people. Their life and enthusiasm is something we cannot afford to be without both now and in the future. We therefore owe a great debt to the Bishop of Carlisle, the National Youth Officers and their staff, and to all those who have worked to produce this report, in the hope that it will stimulate further work in this area.

At the risk of repeating points that are emphasised in the main body of the text, let me offer two reflections and identify four key challenges to the Church.

My first reflection is that, despite what some social commentators have said, young people are not unspiritual. It is true that many of them have turned away from institutional forms of Christianity. Ours is a culture where, as many have pointed out, belief is often kept separate from the question of belonging to a Church. Yet the quest for spiritual realities, particularly those rooted in experience is common to many. Such a quest sometimes expresses itself in mysticism or in a fascination with anything supernatural. Sometimes too it focuses on issues to do with justice, human rights or concern for the environment. For others their searching takes them to Taizé or Greenbelt. But what all these have in common is that they lead out of, or into, profoundly spiritual questions – and the Church must be ready to respond to them.

My second reflection is that, in the Church of England, we are uniquely placed amongst the Churches of this country to reach out to its young people. Whether in our schools, or amongst choir members and bell-ringers; whether in youth groups or through marriage or baptism preparation, the way we have fashioned our ministry gives us natural contact with hundreds of thousands of young adults every week. Sadly, as this report so graphically shows, along with many other similar groups run by schools and local authorities, the numbers of those involved in our youth groups and uniformed organisations has been going down for some time. But, by concentrating on percentage decline, there is a danger that we end up underestimating the very considerable opportunities still open to us.

I was reminded of these recently when I paid an official visit to the Navy and saw something of the work of its chaplains. In the course of the few days I spent with them I was told that the average age of those on board an aircraft carrier is twenty three – and on a frigate is twenty one. Many of the soldiers I met just before Christmas in Bosnia were in the age range covered by this report. Likewise our chaplains in the prison service have considerable experience working with this age group, and have their own stories to tell about how lives that seemed to promise so little, have blossomed given the right kind of care and encouragement.

From my experiences of visiting churches in different parts of the world I am in no doubt that many of them would be overjoyed to have this much contact with this age group. It is a privilege we must not squander and it has profound challenges to put to us, as this report shows, with regard to worship, resources, training and evangelism

First, worship. The report is right to point out that the youth scene is characterised by a ferment of experimentation. The development of many different styles of Alternative Worship Services shows just how creative this age group can be – and how unwise it is to believe a caricature that all that these are about are 'Raves in the Nave'. The challenge here is to foster such experimentation with flexibility and accountability whilst at the same time finding ways to help the members of those services remain a part of the Church of England, and so allow their vitality and new insights to benefit us all.

Second, financial resources. Whilst no one can quantify in monetary terms the huge amount of voluntary time and effort that goes into the care of young people, nevertheless the lack of financial investment into this area of the Church's life is a worrying feature of our life at national, diocesan and parochial level. Only with the latter are there some signs of changes for the better. An increasing number of PCCs are finding ways of employing youth workers on a full- or part-time basis. Nor are these only confined to 'rich' congregations thanks to organisations like the Church Army and to the generosity of the Church Urban Fund and other grant-making bodies. In addition, many Churches are spending more on providing materials and training opportunities for their leaders, whether through Spectrum or other courses. These trends are encouraging but, at a time when so many local authorities have been cutting back on their youth provision – and we are so often tempted to follow suit – it is vital, as this report suggests, to look afresh at our budgets to see if they reflect properly our commitment to this age group.

Third, training. Historically much of our youth work has been done by those with little or no specialist training and there is still a temptation in some quarters to believe that 'anything goes'. I would not wish for one moment to belittle the achievements of those who have worked faithfully over the years with no particular training, but the Children Act, along with other legislation, requires us to approach all our youth work with a new degree of professionalism. Too often our youth workers have been under-valued and their skills have gone unrecognised and been left underdeveloped. I therefore welcome the stress of this report in enhancing further the status of youth workers, both paid and voluntary, within our Church's life. I also welcome the way in which courses are developing, frequently on an ecumenical basis, to train people in this field.

Finally, evangelism, and I include with this a theology of 'The Church as home'. I began this foreword with the story of the development of my own Christian faith. The late teens and early twenties are still a crucial period for many people in their spiritual pilgrimage and, as in my own case, it is often their peers who help them on that journey. But young people with little or no experience of Church life will only listen to the message of the faith if they are welcomed into our Churches and made to feel that they belong. We must recall that the Church is always 'one generation away from extinction'. If all Church members, young and old alike, do not hand on the incomparable riches of Christ then we shall be failing Our Lord. As the Preface to the Declaration of Assent states – We are called upon, as a

Church, to proclaim the faith 'afresh in each generation'. My hope is that this report will stimulate us to do precisely that so that many thousands of young people, in this second half of the Decade of Evangelism, may come to find, as I did over forty years ago, the excitement, challenge and satisfaction of a living relationship with Christ.

✠ George Cantuar

✠ George Cantuar
Archbishop of Canterbury

Members of the Working Party

The Bishop of Carlisle	Chairman
Maxine Green	Secretary to the Working Party National Youth Officer (from January 1995)
Peter Ball	National Youth Officer (from October 1994)
Gill Brentford	General Synod member
Anthony Chandler	Head Teacher, The Scout Association Nominee
Graham Cray	Board of Mission nominee
John D'Souza	Young Adult Forum
Christine Dyer	Diocesan Youth Officer, Derby Diocese
Colin Fletcher	Domestic Chaplain to the Archbishop of Canterbury
Anne Foreman	National Youth Officer (From January 1991 to October 1994)
Shivaun Heath	Young Adult Forum
Walter James	Board of Education
Neil Kendra	Head of Community and Youth Studies, University College St Martin, Lancaster
Ian Knox	VCE Committee, Board of Education and General Synod member
Phil Moon (Originally nominated as Head of CYFA until August 1994)	Representing CYFA (Church Youth Fellowships Association)
Jenny Nightingale	Chair, General Synod Youth Affairs Forum, General Synod member
Anne Richards	Mission Theology Secretary, Board of Mission
Jonathan Roberts	National Youth Officer (From September 1992 to July 1994)
John Thomas	Committee for Black Anglican Concerns
Pete Ward	Archbishop's Adviser on Youth Ministry and Tutor of Oxford Youth Works

Working Party
Terms of Reference

The purpose of the Working Party is to write and publish a substantial report on the extent, nature and purpose of youth work in the Church of England which parishes, deaneries and dioceses can use as a reference point when considering work with young people. The report should:

a)   Offer a theological framework for youth work.

b)   Provide examples of the range of work encompassed by the term 'youth work' in the Church of England.

c)   Identify ways that Church youth work can engage in the lives of young people and develop and nurture their faith.

d)   Indicate the way in which Church youth work relates to other agencies in the same field.

e)   Advise about ways that volunteer and paid youth workers can be recruited, supported and trained and their ministry amongst young people recognised.

Working Parties have been established for each of the above aspects of *Youth A Part*.

A survey of current youth work undertaken in parishes has been conducted and evidence gained for this is being collated by staff of the National Society.

Youth A Part will be presented to General Synod during their meeting in July 1996.

A racial attack occurs every half hour. People from ethnic minorities are 60 times more likely to be targets. Asian women and children suffer the most. Those with disabilities are more likely to suffer abuse (67 per cent) than the able bodied.

Whilst children and young people, like adults, experience inequality according to social class, gender, ethnicity and disability, they also experience inequality in terms of power because of their status as minors.

The way it is, Children's Society

I feel that the Church must recognise discrimination in its many forms whether it is racial, cultural, sexual or religious based. Also to face it head on and to recognise the problems this can bring about. The Church has to show that discrimination of any kind is unacceptable and totally un-Christ-like.

Susan Bruno, young person, Diocese of Chelmsford

1.6   If the Church is to be open and responsive, it must start with information and understanding, go on to address steps that can be taken to challenge situations and finally assess the effectiveness of any strategies taken. This means that the concern for injustice has to be matched by actions to challenge the injustice. In the words of a person at a Report consultation, 'Don't talk about it, Do it' (see paragraph 2.31).

A recent conference in Birmingham of the Black Anglican Youth suggested the following:

1.   Acknowledging our skills base

The good news is that there is a future for our Church – look at our many gifts and talents.

2.   Telling it like it is

The issue is not simply about Black and Asian participation, it is about young people participation.

3.   Changing the way it is

An open mind creates an open heart which brings dialogue and therefore communication and finally results in breaking down ignorance.

- By allowing young people to have this freedom in the knowledge of having the confidence of the congregation this may lead to comments of 'boring, too traditional, etc' being eliminated.

9

4.   Making it happen

In making things happen and things change, we need to examine ourselves, our motives, our part in making it happen . . . Without community
(congregation) support which can be through prayer and their commitment things may not change.

Challenging the Church

> *There can be few other areas, if any in this country (except, possibly,*
> *in the field of housing and homelessness) where the Church of*
> *England is seen to work alongside non-Church agencies and statu-*
> *tory authorities to the extent that it does in the Youth Service. This*
> *experience of a collaborative and co-operative Church doing justice,*
> *loving mercy and walking humbly instead of arrogantly is one that*
> *ought not lightly or wantonly to be damaged or distorted. It certainly*
> *ought not to be discarded. For the Church to withdraw from the world*
> *into an ecclesiastical ghetto or comfort zone is at all times and in all*
> *places a deeply sinful response to the world. To withdraw from this*
> *service to young people in an age in which their vulnerability and dis-*
> *advantage has increased exponentially would be close to betrayal.*
> *There has always been a temptation for the religious to be so wrapped*
> *up in their own rabbinical and levitical activities that they pass by on*
> *the other side of suffering humanity's non-religious needs. That siren*
> *call has to be resisted.*
>
> Professor Walter James, Member of the Working Party

1.7   The Church is challenged not only by tradition, theology and
current interpretation of the gospels, but also by the different political
practices of the time. One concern is with the reduction in Local Authority
funding for youth work. Although at one level this offers an opportunity for
the Church to be involved, at another level the Church's involvement may
be to fight cuts in provision to the members of its parishes. Members in
the Church must research this carefully to help make the most appropriate, caring and responsible Christian response.

It can be argued that the Church is most profoundly challenged by the
many young people who are part of society and care passionately for the
wider issues that affect them and the world. Many young people hold deep
convictions; many are concerned for the environment and the world.

> *I want a society which is fair and there is equality, peace and*
> *harmony — I would like to go into politics but I don't know if I am*
> *right or left. (Age 18)*

I don't think homelessness is looked at in the right way – the Government seem to say that it's the problems of the individuals and they shouldn't do anything about it. (Age 16)

I want the world to be safe for my daughter. I want her to be able to paddle on the beach like I could when I was little.

Battersea, quoted in *The way it is*, Children's Society

This energy and enthusiasm for a better world is at the heart of Christian teaching. Opportunities to engage with young people in this debate can be used not just to make the teaching of the Church more relevant and sympathetic to young people but to work for a better world (see paragraph 2.3)

Young people in a 'post-modern' world

. 1.8   Young people's culture is one of continual change and rapid transitions. No sooner is a song fashionable and older people come to hear of it than a newer song takes its place. Videos, expertly produced by film companies and accurately marketed for maximum effect, use multiple quick-changing images and music. A concert is an experience of being part of a large group with flashing lights, heightened excitement and a total assailing of the senses. Christianity is one voice in the middle of this deluge of information and images.

> *The world looks suspiciously like a 20 channel satellite TV with a madman holding the remote control: before you have time to make sense of the story, the screen beams other images, to be replaced with yet other images, before you begin to know what they are images of; and all comes from nowhere and melts into nowhere again.*
>
> Zygmunt Bauman (1994)

⌐ 1.9   In the world of post-modernism there is a fragmentation and disassociation which lacks any unity or coherence. In this world, Alvin Toffler (1973) describes 'Personal Security Zones' (PSVs), places which are similar and predictable in an ever-changing world, (see paragraph 2.12) for example MacDonalds, which remains the same whether it is in Budapest, Johannesburg, London or New York. Nick Mercer writes, 'There was a time when churches were PSVs. But now they are menacingly unpredictable, even in the Home Counties' (1995).

Mercer also relates how belief has become a commodity to people, who say, 'I buy into a belief and use it to feel good. If it doesn't make me feel good, then why bother to buy into it?'.

1.10   The constant, fragmented chunks of experience together with the
TV culture have numbed the human response. Mercer states, 'We have to
cope with so many emotions in so short a space of time each day. The TV
culture and sound bite sensations have coarsened the human spirit'.

In the post-modern world, all meaning is relative, and there is a constant
switching from one set of reference points to another the unifying 'truth'
of the gospels competes in the market place of many meanings.

1.11   It is on this stage that the Church and Christians have to operate.
Even though this is a difficult task, there are essential elements within the
gospels and Church tradition which make Christianity as relevant as ever
in helping people to have lives with real meaning.

Mercer (1995) writes, 'A vibrant corporate spiritual life, whether charismatic, Toronto-blessed, Anglo-catholic or Alternative worship, points to
human creatureliness and the otherness of God which post-modernity
denies but which our image of Godness yearns after'.

The 'gap' between youth cultures and church cultures

*A young person coming to our church for the first time was com-
pletely lost and obviously very worried about when to stand up, sit
down, whether he could go up to communion, and was puzzled by the
strangeness of the words and ideas. The only link from his 'normal
world' to this new world of the church service was me, and as I looked
at the ritual afresh through his eyes it appeared strange and unreal.
Although this young man comes to church occasionally it is still very
uncomfortable for him. I was thinking that he would no more listen
to classical or organ music at home than he would sit still for an hour.
I couldn't help wondering whether we were expecting him to do all the
adjusting and whether there wasn't something more that we could do
as a church.*

Youth worker

1.12   Many people writing to the report told of this difference between
what happens in many churches and what young people are familiar with
in other things they do. They spoke of the gap between the church culture
and young people's culture. There was also a real desire being expressed
as to how this gap can be bridged and a frustration and a sadness that
many young people are unable to work through this and end up 'voting
with their feet'.

Young people's attendance at church

1.13   Research done by Francis and Lankshear shows that the number of young people who are attending church is falling.

The total Sunday attendance at Anglican Churches amongst 14- to 17-year-olds is 60,739.

This represents a drop of 34.9 per cent since 1987.

Amongst 18- to 21-year-olds the total Sunday attendance is 33,955, a drop of 34.1 per cent since 1987.

The total attendance of 22-5 year olds is 53,405 (there are no comparative figures for this age group in 1987).

1.14   This is not just a problem that churches are facing; the research goes on to show how other organisations are experiencing drops in attendance. Church-based Scouts and Guides also have decreased by 15.8 per cent (14-to 17-year-olds) and 20.4 per cent (18- to 21-year-olds) between 1987 and 1993.

This drop in numbers is not limited to church services; church-based youth work has experienced a decline of 35.4 per cent with the 14-to 17-year-olds and 40.2 per cent among the 18-21-year-olds in the same period. Similar patterns of declining attendance can also be found in secular organisations. The questions this poses for those in the Church are firstly, what is happening to bring about this drop in attendance and secondly, how can we make our churches and other initiatives more attractive to young people so that they have the opportunity to come to know the gospel?

1.15   The reasons given to the report for dropping out of the Church corresponded closely to those given in Statistical Bulletin Issue No. 1/95 published by the Department for Education on 'Young People's Participation in the Youth Service'.

Reasons given for dropping out of the Youth Service

I grew out of it

Not interested in the activities on offer

I was too busy

I was bored

Poor facilities

Badly organised

I dislike the people who go

1.16   There are general factors which influence young people joining groups and organisations in the same way as they did in the early part of the twentieth century.

Given this, there are still steps which can be taken to make the Church a more attractive place for young people.

Church and Christian cultures

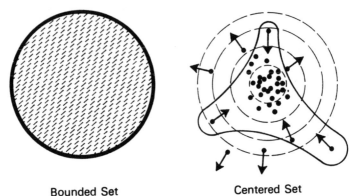

Bounded Set   Centered Set

1.17   One suggestion is to look at Church culture to see what principal elements exist there and to find how they inhibit young people.

Monica Hill in *Entering the Kingdom*, using Professor G. Hiebert's analysis, states that there are two views of Church-based work with young people.

> *For many years Western missionaries have tended to look at things in a certain way. Theirs is a 'bounded set' mentality. This means that they create a category — called a 'bounded set' — by listing its essential characteristics, and thereby giving it a clear boundary. They then devote considerable effort to defining and maintaining this boundary. This forces them to see all within the set as having uniform and essential characteristics. Furthermore the set they have established is static and unchanging. Following this line, they define 'Christian' in terms of a set of essential, measurable, definitive characteristics — like right doctrine plus right polity plus right action. According to their definition they know those who are with them — 'sharing our sameness' — and those who are outside — 'not our kind'. They have an 'ecclesiastical' approach to evangelism. It involves getting people to cross their boundary and conform to their category's essential, measurable characteristics. They make this their task worldwide; to multiply themselves. The result is 'mission planted churches'.*

Nowadays many dynamic groups all over the world are coming to see things differently: the thriving independent churches of Asia, Africa and Latin America, the many 'breakaway movements that were once part of these static Western 'bounded sets'. They define membership standards loosely – if at all. Their preoccupation is with the centre: lifting up Jesus Christ. They view people in terms of their relation to the centre. Some may be far removed from the centre, but moving towards it. This means that they are within the 'centred set'. Others may be much nearer the centre, but moving away from it. They don't belong. The 'centred set' only consists of those moving towards its centre. The centre is the focus, not the boundary, although the boundary conversion is necessary. Suffice it to say, maintaining the boundary is not important, provided the centre is kept in clear focus. Hence wide variation is tolerated by the set. The concern is not with uniformity, but with movement towards the centre. Some are far away, coming from another direction. Nearness is the dimension of biblical knowledge, spiritual growth and commitment to Jesus Christ who is the Centre. This means that the set is dynamic; something which is always happening.

1.18   John Richardson, a community worker, is seeking to use the centred set model of work in a project in Preston. This model moves from the bounded set model, where the work

1. is prescribed – laid down from above and is reactive

2. is not interventionist

3. has an area of practice which is already determined and defined,

to a centred set model, where the work

1. is proscribed – current practice is interrogated and proactive

2. is biased to the oppressed

3. is constantly changing.

This new outreach model suggests that we could be moving towards a dramatically different kind of helping. Without abandoning traditional approaches, the youth and community worker will constantly be reaching out to help others with creative, innovative community changing approaches.

The essential element of this is the concept of 'community'. . . . . The Latin communis consists of 'com', which means together, and 'munis', *meaning to be of service. The real community is ready to be of service together.*

Young people's access to Church

1.19   Within Church culture the bounded set may refer to those within the Church who want to keep it the same, who want to manage the work within the Church to ensure that there are certain standards. However, this means that those who are outside the Church may see this as a pressure to conform and may not be prepared to do so. Those who are not prepared to conform will not have access to the Church's teaching and to the gospels.

A church may fail to recognise that they are 'bounded'. Those within the church may think that they are welcoming and open and that the church is accessible.

> *Ask an adult congregation 'Is this parish church accessible to young people?' The answer is of course 'Yes, because they only have to walk in through the door.' Ask the same adults if they have ever avoided using public toilets even if they have needed to and there will be stories about why they couldn't use them on particular occasions, even though they were 'accessible'. The issue of accessibility highlights the differences between Church culture and youth cultures. The barriers young people have to climb are similar in terms of experience to adults turning away from public toilets. Who might you meet in there? Does the environment match my values and standards? Will I feel embarrassed?*

Denis Tully, Diocesan Youth Officer, Southwell Diocese

1.20   In an effort to make the Church more accessible there is a temptation for those in the Church to see young people's culture from the outside and try to imitate this in services and youth work. However, if we try to capture a single vision of 'what young people want' and try to reproduce it by sparkling up a service or putting on a youth disco with dry ice and flashing lights, we may miss other young people who do not find this appealing. Similarly, if we offer a chance to explore Celtic spirituality, Christian meditation and silence, this may not appeal to other groups or individuals (see paragraph 4.2).

In short, there is no more a single youth culture than there is a single elderly culture. For young people to feel to feel spiritually at home they need the opportunities to create meaningful acts of service and of worship with those in the rest of the church. They also need to know that their voices count and have a say in the decisions of the church. This involves changes to how many churches work at the moment to ensure that young people are consulted, encouraged and involved.

This consultation and negotiation has to be done in a church which recognises its legacy of being white, male, middle-class and with a tradition of being in control. Opportunities need to be made to understand rather than be encumbered by this history.

A diocesan youth officer writes 'A question the congregation can ask is, does it want young people in church or does it welcome young people into the church?' This is crucial in determining how the Church approaches the whole question of access.

Working in different contexts

1.21   If you were to ask twenty people 'What is youth work' you would get twenty different answers, drawing on people's experience and training. Although there are many different ways to describe youth work, there are some fundamental principles which undergird good practice in work with young people.

Undergirding principles of youth work

1. Education – to encourage and resource young people to develop understanding, values, skills and behaviour.

2. Empowerment – to give opportunities to young people to equip themselves to take control and manage their lives.

3. Equal Opportunities – to ensure that young people are not discriminated against and to help them to challenge and oppose prejudice.

4. Participation – to give opportunities for young people to develop and grow by offering and resourcing a whole range of activities in which they can be actively involved.

Statement of purpose for the Youth Service agreed at the Second Ministerial Conference, November 1990

1.22   Youth work is about a process. It is the act of working things out, being in groups, taking part in activities. One of the functions of the youth worker is to help young people reflect on these experiences and use them to develop and grow. Consequently it is extremely important to understand the influences on young people. They may be due to growing up at this particular time in the twentieth century or growing up in different environments. An inner city parish in an Urban Priority Area will have different tensions and advantages to a rural setting; much work has been done within these two areas and some is described below.

Rural youth work

1.23   The difficulties experienced by young people living in small villages was highlighted in 1964 by the 'Youth Service Development Council'. This work is widely recognised as being necessary and important, but all rural provision is expensive per capita because of scarcity and sparcity. Without investment into this work young people are often deprived of a range of opportunities readily available to their peers living in urban areas.

> I am reminded all too frequently that although the young people from my village have transport to and from school, and a late bus several evenings during the week which enables them to participate in after school activities, once they are home from school they become totally dependent on adults for transport.
>
> Peter Ball, National Youth Officer and Member of the Working Party

Peter Ball adds that 'Churches, voluntary organisations, local authorities, charitable trusts and central government must build on the valuable experience of joint working to ensure wider provision of good quality youth work'.

1.24   There are a number of projects sponsored by the Church, or where the Church is working in partnership with young people in a rural setting.

> Churches Outreach Project – Diocese of Leicester
>
> The Project's aim is 'to research, identify, initiate, develop and support work of the Church in smaller communities'.
>
> The project was developed and operated by two professionally qualified youth and community development workers. The project arose out of a concern for the apparent lack of contact between young people in their adolescent years living in more rural villages of South Leicestershire and the life of their parish church. The project has been in existence since January 1991.
>
> The C.O.P. works with Christians of all denominations and links in with local regional, and national rural and/or youth organisations.
>
> Examples of practice:
>
> *   Development of youth group for small parish church
>
> *   Residential narrow boat trips (in conjunction with Centre Light

Trust) with rural, isolated young people and groups

* Production of various publications

* Development of a resource base to support and resource voluntary church-based youth and community workers

* Talking and spending time with individual voluntary youth workers

* Pastoral support of young people in transition to adulthood, struggling to come to terms with issues such as parental bereavement and family break-ups

* Personal and social education of young people from within a Christian framework

* Encouraging young people to explore their spirituality, the Christian message and the relevance of the church today

* Work with young people with special needs using an integrated model

* Teenage work within Holiday Bible Club settings

* Detached street work with young people

* Training and leading workshops for youth workers and ministers

* Encouraging the statutory sector to develop links with voluntary church-based work

There are other interesting initiatives taking place in rural youth work. There are bus projects where a bus kitted out for youth work tours small villages on a regular basis and builds up regular groups in different areas. The Archbishop of Canterbury dedicated a bus for this work in Norfolk in June 1994, in response to youth work being impossible because of the lack of suitable people to lead the work, no premises or no resources.

1.25   What is crucial about rural youth work is to appreciate that the countryside is not necessarily an idyll to young people, some of whom have to manage problems such as homelessness, bullying and family break-up in isolation and with limited support.

1.26 ⁴ David Popham, writing in *Country Way*, (Summer 1995), gives some advice to those working in rural youth work. He says that the work may cover a wider age band than urban work, attract fewer young people and need to take into account the specific nature of rural work (not be an urban transplant – a homegrown way of working responds to the interests

of the young people involved and the skills of the worker). He also highlights the importance of vision – reliance on prayer and guidance from the
Holy Spirit, honesty – being open about the work and its Christian base;
and commitment – to get on and do, and be ready to take risks.

1.27   As well as the larger projects it is important to note that there are
thousands of parishes where members of the church – adults or young
people – befriend, encourage and work with young people. 'All of us can
do something worthwhile – get to know one or two local young people,
and help them to realise how much we value them as people. Church life,
worship and organisation too must be more responsive to the presence
(or is it absence) of young people in our midst', (Peter Ball).

Urban youth work

1.28   The pressures for urban youth are much less hidden than those in
rural youth work. Many young people in cities or large towns face bleak
futures of unemployment, living in poor housing, and with very little hope.
The Church has a ministry to these young people not least as an organisation that they are part of, which can challenge and change their society.

1.29   The Church Urban Fund has been instrumental in providing
money for many initiatives.

Brief Guide to Projects funded by the Church Urban Fund

Urban Regeneration	job creating initiatives
Poverty and Unemployment	tackling the effects of unemployment
Health	health care in the community
Housing	addressing homelessness
Social Care	service provision
Community Work	supported development of communities
Education and Young People	includes youth work
Order and Law	informal and formal justice
Interfaith	practical collaboration and discussion
Church Buildings	opening up for community use
Faith in the City	general matters arising from the report
Evangelism	deliberate outreach
Supporting the Ministry	lay ministry, parish administrators, etc.

An example of a particular project is the St Thomas' Project, Garretts Green, Diocese of Birmingham. Garretts Green is an outer city Urban Priority Area, mainly council housing with high levels of unemployment. The objective of the project is to respond to the physical, emotional and spiritual needs of the community. In particular the lack of youth facilities and the problems with unemployment are areas the project aims to address. The project hopes to establish a base where advice, support, friendship and constructive activities are easily available.

1.30   As well as the larger projects, there are a number of small initiatives which are often parish based and specifically aimed towards young people, where the same focus on relationships and care of young people is as important as in a rural setting.

Community-based work

Foxton Youth and Community Centre, Diocese of Blackburn

This centre runs a junior club and does specific activities for young people. However, it is part of a larger community project where there are opportunities for all ages. As well as the wider aims of youth work the project stresses the idea of community and building permanent, stable trusting relationships between the helpers and those who use the centre. 'The vast majority of the young people who attend the club are experiencing some form of deprivation, which can be through lack of money, stimulation, attention or solid, fulfilling relationships with the people around them. The impact the club has on the lives of these young people is very apparent to anyone who has a good level of contact with children in the Avenham area. Even in the sixteen months that I have been a staff member I have seen a remarkable improvement in the behaviour, interactions and social skills of these young people.'

(Centre worker)

This project is part of a Christian outreach to the community and is helping young people to learn to support and care for each other. Another community-based project is the Bilsthorpe Community Project Proposal, which aims to explore the identity that had previously been focused on the now closed pit and use the sense of community that was so strong as a resource for developing a new community. The project proposal follows a developmental faith model and sees the community identity as being bound with the spiritual identity of the community.

Conclusion

1.31   The time and place that we live in define our lives to a great extent. If models of work with young people are to be effective, they have to build on the current experience of young people and they have to take into account the fragmented images and values of the post-modern world.

This means that workers, young or old, within the Church need a good understanding of the issues that young people face, and they need to be aware of specific problems relating to where they live and the age and situation of each person (see paragraph 2.28).

There is no formula for this work, although other people's good practice can be invaluable in working out possible projects or activities. Keystones in the work include relationships which are built on an integrity and trust arising from the gospels and the model of Christ; the ethic of loving one's neighbour; and a respect for young people which communicates their value in the Church and in Church work.

If young people are taken seriously, respected and truly valued, the 'gap' between Church culture and youth culture will decrease and close quite naturally.

2

A Theology for Youth Work

Youth work and the mission of god

The nature of the Church's mission

2.1   Youth work needs to be understood as a dimension of the Church's mission. Mission is a characteristic which defines the Church because the God that Christians worship and serve is the God who revealed himself to us in mission and whose mission to the world continues today.

> Mission has its origin in God. God is a missionary God, a God who crosses frontiers towards the world. In creation God was already the God of mission, with his Word and Spirit as 'Missionaries' (Genesis 1.2–3). God likewise sent his incarnate Word, his Son, into the world. And he sent his Spirit at Pentecost. Mission is God giving up himself, his becoming (hu)man, his laying aside of his divine prerogatives and taking our humanity, his moving into the world, in his Son and Spirit.
>
> David Bosch, p. 239 (1980)

2.2   The Church's mission to people, young and old, is derived from and shaped by God's mission. Because he crossed frontiers for our salvation we cross frontiers, in partnership with him, to bear his salvation to others.

> Set us free, O God,
> to cross barriers for you,
> as you crossed barriers for us
> in Jesus Christ our Lord. Amen.
>
> Brother Bernard, Society of St Francis

The Church's tasks in mission

> The Church's task is to serve the mission of God in the world.
> Advisory Council for the Church's Ministry (1987) 22, pp. 27–8

2.3   The Church of England bases its training of ordained ministers on the belief that the Church is essentially a missionary community. The ministers are to be leaders and enablers in the mission of the whole people of God. This mission is seen as a twofold task:

● to proclaim the creative activity of God. That God has created and continues to sustain everything that exists.

● to proclaim the redemptive activity of God. That in Jesus Christ he has acted in human history to restore a creation broken by human sin.

In this task it follows, and by its nature seeks to conform to, the work of God – through Jesus Christ and by the Holy Spirit – in and for the world, in order to bring the world to its proper relation to God.

Advisory Council for the Church's Ministry (1987) 22, pp. 27–8

2.4   The creative and redemptive aspects of God's mission meet in the person and work of Christ. Their point of integration is in him. He is the world's origin, coherence and purpose. His cross is the source of the world's redemption (Colossians 1.15–20).

Because of Christ's work of redemption, the mission of God points forward to the restoration of the whole creation. His resurrection (1 Corinthians 15.20) and the work of the Spirit (Roman 8.23) anticipate this restoration. Christians therefore live and work 'between the times' as signs of God's kingdom in the world. They look forward to the time when reconciliation is complete; when through judgement all things are made new (Revelation 20.11 – 21.6).

The integration of the Church's mission

2.5   In essence, mission is the proclamation of Christ and his kingdom by word and deed. Proclamation is not only the action of preaching of the gospel. It is also the demonstration, which the Church is called to make, of the nature and extent of Christ's salvation, so that all people have the opportunity to see it, to understand it, to respond to it and experience it.

Youth work should express the same integration of creation and redemption which is seen in the work of Christ. It should therefore be understood and attempted in a holistic way. Categories such as social action, evangelism, social and personal development, and pastoral care are not adequate in themselves. They must neither be set in competition to one another nor be simply added together; they need to find their point of integration in relation to the mission of God, particularly as it is made known to us in the gospel of Christ.

Youth work is mission in the context of culture

2.6　　The gospel of Christ is unchanging. It is this gospel which 'the Church is called upon to proclaim afresh in each generation' (Declaration of Assent). However, all the Church's mission is set in a specific context and culture. It is rooted in Christ's Incarnation and initiated by the Spirit.

The Incarnation is unique. It is the quintessential missionary act of God in which he has taken our human nature once for all. It is essential as the context and the precondition for the atonement, in which Christ's death breaks down the ultimate barrier of our alienation from our Maker.

The Incarnation was also specific to the culture of first century Palestine, not as a limitation but as a demonstration and guarantee that the gospel of Christ could take equally specific root within each culture and era. We do not have to become first century Jews to become Christians (see Acts 15.1–35). It is the Holy Spirit who leads and equips the Church for this task, just as he led and equipped Christ.

2.7　　Youth work must relate directly to the era of culture in which it is set and to adolescence and young adulthood as stages of life. It must engage seriously with young people's questions and with contemporary issues concerning young people.

The Church is called to proclaim the gospel and teach the Christian tradition to each generation of young people, but it must also approach the gospel with the questions which arise out of young people's experience. As they discover Christ for themselves, young people will form their own opinions of the way in which the gospel is brought to them, and they will have insights which are essential to the Church's growth.

> Every evangelist runs the risk that the seed of the gospel, once planted in the life of a new believer, may grow into a dynamic force which threatens to overthrow the very status quo in which the evangelist finds comfort and rest.
>
> Jim Wallis (1976)

2.8　　The Church's work among young people combines continuity with change. It begins with its responsibility to pass on its faith to the next generation:

> and what you have heard from me through many witnesses entrust to faithful people who will be able to teach others as well.
>
> 2 Timothy 2:2

It continues with the responsibility to be open to change, as the Church listens to the Spirit of Christ in the young. Youth work needs to give young people opportunities to hold a mirror up to the Church, so that the Church can look at itself and not fall into complacency. Without this willingness to listen, Christian mission can be trapped in a timewarp and become ineffective. The Church has a delicate balance to keep between its responsibility to pass on the faith it has received, and its responsibility to listen as each new generation makes its own response to Christ. As it does this, young people can be encouraged to further the missionary dynamic where change is required by faithfulness to the kingdom.

Western culture

2.9   The gospel cannot be made known apart from culture; but the attitude of the gospel to any particular culture will always be a combination of affirmation and challenge.

> This conference recognises that culture is the context in which people find their identity; affirms that the gospel judges every culture challenging some aspects of the culture while endorsing others for the benefit of the church and society.
>
> Lambeth Conference, 1988, Resolution 22

The primary context of youth work at the turn of the twentieth century is a profound shift in culture as 'modernity', the characteristic form of western culture developed from the Enlightenment, changes its shape and focus. This period of transition is called by many 'post-modernity'.

> There is a widely shared sense that Western ways of seeing, knowing and representing have irreversibly altered in recent times: but there is little consensus over what this might mean or what direction Western Culture is now taking. Has modernity really come to a close or has it simply undergone a change of appearance?"
>
> Jon R. Snyder in Vattimo (1988)

> Quite unprecedented social and cultural shifts are occurring that fundamentally question the whole edifice of modernity.
>
> David Lyon (1994)

2.10   Religious institutions, like their secular counterparts, are undergoing a substantial crisis of confidence. The overall picture is complex, with secularisation, pluralism, institutional religious decline and spiritual awakening. However, it is clear that religion and spirituality will have a vital part to play in the shaping of the next era of culture.

> We will search for an ethical vocabulary of duties as well as rights; for a new language of environmental restraint; for communities of shared

responsibility and support; for relationships more enduring than those of temporary compatibility; and for that sense which lies at the heart of the religious experience, that human life has meaning beyond the self. These are themes central to the great religious traditions, and we will not have to reinvent them.

Jonathan Sacks (1991)

2.11   The primary frontier which needs to be crossed in mission to young people is not so much a generation gap as a profound change in the overall culture. Today's young people will have to find ways of discipleship which are not familiar to adults in the Church. Not all that older generation's attempt to pass on will be helpful.

The world that our parents knew is not the world we live in today; nor is our world any sure guide to the way in which our children will live and love and work.

Charles Handy (1995)

Adolescence and culture

2.12   The emergence of youth culture and the recognition of adolescence as a distinctive stage in life between childhood and adulthood took place in the 1950s as the combined result of earlier puberty, extended compulsory education and independent spending power. There have always been tensions between succeeding generations, but the more sharply defined concept of a generation gap came from that same cultural and social development. Adolescent popular culture still defines itself against adult culture to a considerable extent; but, in reality, youth culture has been shaped much more significantly by the changes overtaking western culture as a whole.

The society young people find themselves in is one shaped, planned and run by adults: nothing very new about that. But this society, being run by adults is significantly different from the one in which those same adults – you and me – experienced their own adolescence.

Anne Foreman Eagles Wings Conference 1994

2.13   Youth culture no longer has the unity of direction which it appeared to have in the 1950s to 1970s. Nor, since the 1980s, is it necessarily counter-cultural. The 1980s was a time emphasising commodities and style. The youth market created parallel ways for young people to participate: subcultures rather than counter culture. Now, the peer group still has great influence, but the fragmentation of the adult culture is echoed in youth culture by a diversity of styles, groups and interests which are continually in flux.

At the same time, adults are experiencing a loss of hope in progress and in the inevitability of a better future. As a consequence much adult culture is trapped in an ongoing adolescent search for identity and has developed characteristics that were once unique to teenage.

> *The natural instability of youth, once viewed as simply a stage of life, is now projected upon much of adult society, presented as a normative attitude toward life. In other words, age no longer denotes personal stability and maturity.*
>
> Schulze

> *Nobody is a teenager anymore because everybody is.*
>
> Robert Elms, quoted in Starkey (1995)

2.14   There has been a blurring between the chronological adolescence of youth and the psychological adolescence of much adult culture. Chronological adolescence is a time of transition, exploration and the forming of identity. Paradoxically it may only be the young who can help the Church to find appropriate new forms of *adult* discipleship. In any case youth work will not be able to address the identity crisis of adolescence apart from the larger identity crisis in society as a whole.

Youth work is culture-forming

2.15   As western culture shifts from a modern to a post-modern era, and as many previous certainties are challenged, young people are in the front line of change. Mission in the Decade of Evangelism has to be culture forming, and the young will shape the emerging culture. Whether they shape it with any reference to Christ is the primary challenge for the Church's youth work.

Teenagers in particular are undergoing a double crisis of identity: that of adolescence and that of cultural disintegration. The Church has the opportunity to be alongside them at this strategic moment.

The need for culture formation

2.16   Youth work that is culture forming involves both the reclamation of insights which arise from the gospel but which have been lost to our society, and the search for new insights as the gospel is applied to a new context. This requires the Church to be faithful in passing on the unchanging elements of Christian belief and lifestyle, while at the same time empowering young people to work out the application of those elements for their own context. This has great potential for conflict and misunderstanding. Clergy and youth workers will often be called to fulfil the role of interpreter between young people and others in the Church.

For example, the adult Church has inherited the combined, but at times conflicting, assumptions of Christendom and the Enlightenment. These assumptions are breaking down and can no longer undergird the Church's mission.

Christendom assumes the essentially Christian nature of our society and a natural alliance between the Church and those in authority. The increasing need to develop some form of adult catechumenate (a process of introduction to the Christian Faith like the Alpha Course or the Roman Catholic Rite of Christian Initiation for Adults) is but one reminder that today neither adult nor youth culture is instinctively Christian in either belief or lifestyle. The perceived relationship between religion and power causes great difficulty when there is a growing distrust of institutions in Western culture.

> *The Church is bottom of the confidence ratings for those aged under thirty-five years, but ranks third (out of thirteen) for those aged over fifty years.*
>
> European Values Study 1981–90

2.17   The philosophy and scientific thought of the European Enlightenment has resulted in what Clifford Longley describes as 'a society of unprecedented sophistication, convenience and prosperity.'

The achievements of this society have been unparalleled. No-one would wish to return to a pre-scientific society. However, within the Enlightenment world view, there has been an over-emphasis on the authority of independent human reason. This has lead to the loss of the over-arching awareness of God and of any sense of shared social purpose (see Brian Appleyard, *Understanding the Present*). Trust in many of the Enlightenment values as the basis for a better society has collapsed. It is not surprising that in the wake of this collapse there is a sense of disillusion and cynicism.)

> *Nobody can remember what [society] was supposed to be for.*
>
> Clifford Longley in Sacks, (1995)

2.18   The Church's youth work, in a time of cultural transition, has to be based on the confidence that the gospel is public truth with the capacity to shape a culture, rather than a matter of personal preference. It must operate from an understanding of Christian faith as the basis of an integrated lifestyle rather than as a leisure option. At the same time it has to distance itself from any temptation to impose its beliefs.

Essential Christian contributions to culture

2.19   Young people find themselves facing the challenge of reshaping a culture that is increasingly fragmented. The following seven principles are some of the essential elements of a Christian contribution to an emerging culture.

1. Corporate purpose

We need to regain a sense of purpose and identity in history: rooted in a meaningful past, living purposefully in the present, in the light of a realistic hope for the future.

> *In order to have a sense of who we are, we have to have a notion of how we have become, and of where we are going.*
>
> Charles Taylor (1989)

This provides a realistic alternative to the rootlessness and lack of shared hope which leave our contemporary society in a permanent present of commodities and media images. For a society which is increasingly one-dimensional, the gospel offers a return to a three-dimensional perspective. Western culture turned providence into progress into nihilism (the loss of any shared sense of meaning to life). The gospel creates the possibility of closing the circle.

2. Personal identity

We need to regain an understanding of human identity as that of a person in relationship with others, rather than as that of an independent individual. We only truly know ourselves as persons in relationship with our fellow humans and with God. This is rooted in the doctrine of the Trinity and revealed in the cross of Christ. Through the cross we know that the fundamental reality in the universe is not individual power but sacrificial love.

> *What is needed today is a better understanding of the person, not just as an individual but as someone who finds his or her true being in communion with God and with others, the counterpart of a Trinitarian doctrine of God.*
>
> James Torrance (1989-91)

3. Truth

We need to regain an understanding of truth as both objective and subjective. Objective because the meaning of human existence is revealed in history through the acts of God in Christ; subjective because that truth demands a response and can be personally experienced. Such truth demands commitment and it results in a Christ-like lifestyle. It cannot be discovered either by detached reason or by subjective feeling on their own.

4. Spirituality

We need to restore the place of spirituality in the public as well as the private world, relating it to truth as well as to personal experience. It should be understood as the essential source of character development for a society based on sacrificial love.

> *Worship makes strong demands upon us. It requires no less than we should go out into the world to love, to serve and to care.*
>
> Robin Gill (1992)

Worship, liturgy and spirituality need to be restored to a central place in personal and corporate growth towards maturity.

5. Moral character

We need to regain and restore the faculty of discernment in a media saturated commodity culture. This will involve teaching young people values derived from Christ, as the basis of discernment; but also allowing them to help us to discern all that is good in youth culture which can be brought into the City of God (Revelation 21).

6. Sacrificial community

We need to restore human community in Christ. The reconciling nature of the cross and the new era begun by the resurrection need to be demonstrated in the Church, to show that sacrificial community is possible.

Perhaps the greatest need of our society is the rebuilding of the community. Young people have suffered most from the breakdown of family and society and often combine a longing for relationship with a distrust of it. This cannot be a mere reconstruction of former patterns of community. The Church has both a particular responsibility to affirm marriage as the normal context of parenthood, and to act as extended family for those alienated from their natural families or split apart by social mobility.

Many young people establish their relationships through informal networks. They are not necessarily based on neighbourhoods, let alone parish boundaries. The rebuilding of community will often be within these networks and requires a vision of Church which is not inevitably territorial.

> *Human life is lived in a complex array of networks and the neighbourhoods where people reside may hold only a very minor loyalty.*
>
> Breaking New Ground paragraph 1.7 (1994)

7. Environmental care

We need to re-establish a right relationship to the natural world, developing appropriate patterns of lifestyle in the light of the environmental crisis. In effect this is a restoration of the human calling to be the stewards of the earth, as what is lost in the Fall (Genesis 1–3) is regained in Christ (Romans 5). At this point the biblical gospel and contemporary awareness come closest together.

2.20   These factors, corporate purpose, personal identity, truth, spirituality, moral character, sacrificial community and environmental care are essential building blocks for any emerging social order. They are all dimensions of the mission of God, all arise from the gospel of Christ, and all should be aims of Christian youth work.

Youth work is concerned with personal development

Christ as a model of personal development

2.21   The Church's ministry in education and personal development is founded in its understanding of Christ. Christ is our model for maturity.

2.22   The account of Jesus' visit to Jerusalem with his family in Luke 2.41–52 is of particular importance, as we know nothing else of the time between Jesus' infancy and adulthood. His growth into adulthood, like ours, had physical (including sexual), spiritual, intellectual and social dimensions, amongst others, and found its point of integration in his conscious relationship with God as Father. In the year before formal adulthood Jesus is seen making a personal and spiritual decision over and against his apparent duty to his parents, but not as an evasion of that responsibility. His awareness of God as 'Father', which is expressed in this incident, reaches full expression and confirmation at his baptism (Luke 3.21–23).

The Church's participation in God's mission will involve a similar affirmation of the value and identity of each human person, recognising that the source of this identity is found in relationship with the same Father. Christ's baptism combined the affirmation of his personal identity and value with the anticipation of his sacrificial death. On the same basis, human beings are restored to their true identity through his atonement, and adult maturity is demonstrated by sacrificial love.

If Christ is the decisive model of all humanity, then growth to maturity is characterised by continual learning. Increase in understanding is paralleled by increase in obedience and humility. Jesus' life from his baptism to his crucifixion is the definitive example of this maturing process. His adolescent experience was one formative moment of a lifelong journey. It is not acceptable to understand adolescence as a transitional period before a static adulthood.

2.23   The model provided and taught by Christ challenges any view of youth work as instructing young people *until* they are adults. Christ 'had to become like his brothers and sisters in every respect' (Hebrews 2.17). He was 'made perfect through sufferings' (2.10) and even in Gethsemane 'learned obedience' (5.8). His experience of learning as a youth established an adult pattern of continual learning from his Father. In the same way, he called his disciples to 'be like their teacher'. Christian education of young people only has integrity if it is rooted in a culture of continual adult learning.

Christ's ministry of healing and compassion was offered to all, whatever their response to him; but not ignoring their response. Similarly the Church's youth work will always be committed to the personal development of young people irrespective of their view of Christ; but it can never depart from its understanding that true humanity finds its fulfilment in relationship with him.

Personal and social identity

2.24   The most pressing issue which faces our culture in the area of personal development, is the relationship between personal meaning and social purpose. The two are interdependent. 'Who I am' is related to 'who we are'.

At the root of both personal and social identity is the range of stories humans tell themselves about themselves. A world view is the shared lens through which people with a common culture look at reality. At the heart of any world view is a narrative, a story.

> World views provide the stories through which human beings view reality.
>
> N.T. Wright, chapter 5 (1992)

A sense of personal identity is closely related to the harmony between the stories which individuals tell themselves about themselves and their actual experience of life in their culture.

> A *person's identity is not to be found in behaviour, nor – important though this is – in the reactions of others, but in the capacity to keep a particular narrative going.*

> The individual's biography must continually integrate events which occur in the external world, and sort them out into the ongoing 'story' about the self.
>
> Anthony Giddens (1991)

33

2.25   The Church's work for the personal development of young people has to be understood in the context of its call to form culture. At the very least it is called to show that forms of culture based on the gospel are possible.

Young people's stories and the gospel story

2.26   The gospel can be seen as a 'grand' story meta-narrative which is to be placed alongside the individual's story. It claims to be the story of the origin, purpose, brokenness and future of the whole creation. But this story is not imposed on individuals by God. It is offered through the Incarnation and in the continuing mission of the Church. Claims to truth are not necessarily claims to power.

> *The meta-narrative is not just the story of Jesus, it is the continuing story of the Church, already realised in a final exemplary way by Christ, yet still to be realised universally, in harmony with Christ, and yet differently, by all generations of Christians.*
>
> John Milbank (1990)

2.27   As with all aspects of mission the Church's work with young people is dependent on the witness of the local Christian community.

The story which our culture has told itself for the past two centuries has lost its power to convince. It is no longer seen as obviously true that human ability to reason will lead to inevitable progress. Society has lost both its cohesiveness and its sense of purpose. It is no wonder that many young people lack purpose, identity or even hope for the future.

Ultimately a Christian concern for young people's self identity and personal growth has to be related to the truthfulness or otherwise of the stories they believe about themselves, and the truth of the story of God revealed in Christ. If Christ is the measure of mature humanity, then the Church is called to help young people to relate their own stories within the liberating story of Christ.

Youth work is incarnational

2.28   The Church's mission must always be focused on our understanding of Christ. Christ reveals the true nature of the relationship of God, the Church and the gospel to the world. The nature, needs and dignity of human (in this case young human) life are established by reference to him. His incarnation, ministry, death and resurrection establish both the content of the Church's mission and the methods by which it carries out that mission.

The incarnation reaffirms and underlines the dignity of humankind. It also establishes the pattern of the whole person growing into maturity. Christ is our model of growth 'in wisdom and years, in divine and human favour'. (Luke 2.52).

The concerns for culture outlined in paragraph 2.9 reflect the values of the Triune God. Yet they were not imposed from above but demonstrated in Jesus Christ in solidarity with us. Youth work is also based on incarnation: entering into the young person's world, treating it with discerning respect rather than suspicion; sharing their joys and sorrows; genuinely engaging with their questions while bringing the challenge of Christian discipleship to them.

2.29   Understood in the context of the incarnation, the cross of Christ, which lies at the heart of the biblical gospel, has a double focus.

- At a time when youth culture is characterised by more rage and alienation than ever before, the cross bears testimony to the God who endures alienation, betrayal and injustice. In this limited sense it is the justification of God in the eyes of suffering humanity. This is demonstrated in the four Gospel accounts of the circumstances of the passion.

- At the same time, as clearly stated in Epistles and Gospels, the cross is God's initiative to justify the sinner, young or old, who is alienated from the Creator and in need of an objective atonement.

For many hurting and alienated young people the sense of God's identification with them in the cross may need to be established before the significance of their need of repentance and faith can be established.

The objective work of the cross establishes a security which frees Christians to enter vulnerably into situations of great need. Youth workers need to be able to live in this way to work with those young people who are most alienated from the Church and the rest of society.

2.30   The resurrection is not merely the vindication of Christ but the beginning of a renewed human race and the promise of a renewed creation. The cross and the resurrection together underlie and sustain all Christian mission. Incarnation continues in the power of the Spirit of Christ. The Spirit strengthens youth workers to stay with young people in the times and places of pain without losing hope (Romans 8.18–27).

The Spirit of Christ enables youth workers to enter a culture different from their own. (For an example of such cross-cultural mission see Acts 10.) The Spirit applies the universal Gospel to particular individuals and communities, freeing youth workers from approaches which treat all people the same way. The Spirit also gives gifts to young people in diverse ways (1

Corinthians 12) and opens adult eyes to see the creativity in much of youth culture.

Youth work is relational

2.31   Because youth work is incarnational it must also be relational. It is based on a gospel designed to restore God's relationship with fallen humans and to show that no-one is unreachable. It began with the Creator becoming one of us, unashamed to call human beings his brothers, sisters and friends (Hebrews 2.11, John 15.15). The call to a free, committed discipleship of Christ comes from friend to friend. We communicate through deeds and relationships before we communicate through words. Yet the very integrity of those relationships demands truth expressed in love. Neither tightly controlled systems of discipleship nor purely non-directive approaches will be adequate.

Youth work is a call to discipleship

The need for the gospel

> To bring before our young people the attractiveness of Christ and enable them to contribute their rich gifts to His service.
>
> George Carey, Archbishop of Canterbury

2.32   To summarise what has been said so far: Christian youth work derives its values, goals and methods from the gospel. But to what extent is it necessary to make the gospel itself explicit to young people?

In one sense it is not necessary. The good that Jesus did expressed the character and purpose of the Creator and was often offered regardless of further response. Similarly there are many contexts where for pastoral reasons or for personal or professional integrity it can be inappropriate to make an overt link between the claims of Christ and work being done out of Christian conviction. (This could apply to social work, to local authority youth clubs, to detached projects and to some uniformed organisations).

On the other hand, Jesus openly proclaimed the necessity of repentance and faith and called people to follow him (Mark 1.14ff). Only the gospel has the power to transform lives and form cultures in a way which restores meaning and generates hope. A decision on principle to make no mention of the claims of Christ while at the same time encouraging young people to live out 'Christian' values is a recipe for disillusionment and disappointment. To know the right way to live but to lack the power to live it is a cruel dilemma. A Christian lifestyle can only be lived in the power of the Spirit. In this sense there is no such thing as 'secular' Christian youth work. The answers many young people are seeking cannot be found apart from spirituality. But spirituality is not for its own sake but for the formation of godly character, the restoration of the divine image. Young and old alike are in need of initial and ongoing conversion to Christ.

2.33   However an approach based on conversion alone is equally inadequate. Too often this leads to a dualism: a split existence which divides the spiritual from the remainder of life; or which withdraws new converts from normal society. At a time of cultural change this is especially disastrous as it disables the culture-forming work of the gospel.

The need for discipleship

2.34   Both conversion and personal development are essential, but both need to be integrated in the concept of discipleship. Discipleship is our response to the ongoing call of Jesus to increasing understanding of, and conformity to, God's will. It is sustained in a relationship of faith. God's call to discipleship is accompanied by his commission. We are trusted in the service of Christ and that trust deepens our own faith. Youth work must be characterised by a similar trust of young people if they are to develop as adult disciples of Christ.

At the heart of Jesus' call to discipleship was his proclamation of the kingdom of God as something begun through his own ministry. The call of the kingdom requires individual repentance and faith, but its full extent is that the whole will of God is to be done on earth (Matthew 6.10). If that is not culture forming, then nothing is.

At the heart of the kingdom is a conscious relationship with God as Father expressed in a lifestyle of obedience to the Father's will (Matthew 12.46–50). The Father's will was as much about public issues of justice, power and the poor, as private matters of prayer, honesty and individual generosity.

2.35   This call to discipleship must also have an incarnational setting and be given integrity through personal example. The weaknesses of a failed culture are now being recognised. So any call to repentance needs to be accompanied by a genuine humility which acknowledges how the Church has been compromised by the values of that culture and has itself been part of the problem.

Repentance from the old world view requires a willingness to listen to the young, who will have to develop the new one.

Youth work is community building

2.36   Human identity is established through relationships and the Christian gospel is one of reconciled relationships. So the Church is not only an integral part of the gospel, it is itself an aim of the gospel. It anticipates the renewed humanity of the new heaven and earth. One aim

of Christian youth work must be that young people become fully participating members of Christ's Church. Christianity is always personal, but it
has to be corporate. Christian discipleship cannot be sustained in isolation by young or old.

> *Christian community is not primarily about togetherness . . . togeth-*
> *erness happens, but only as a by-product of the main project of trying*
> *to be faithful to Jesus.*
>
> Stanley Hauerwas and William H. Willimon (1989)

But this raises crucial questions for the local and national Church. It must
be an example of the values it proclaims.

1. It must be a demonstration of discipleship and take particular care with
the way its internal life and relationships handle issues such as, for
example, justice and power.

2. It must be a place accessible to and safe for young people. A community
with permeable boundaries, where movement towards Christ matters more
than the level of commitment achieved; a place where love is indiscriminate.

3. It must be a place where the young are shown that clear convictions
about Christ are compatible with respectful tolerance of the rights and
integrity of those who believe differently.

Conclusion – The inheritance from the past and the Spirit from the future

2.37   The shift in western culture faces the Church with a profound
challenge. Many of our current ways of being the Church will probably
prove inadequate in the emerging society. It is the young people, whom
we help to faith and whom we equip to shape the emerging culture, who
will also need to develop new forms of worship and Church structure.
Those new forms will one day be the mainstream.

The ability to recognise, release and support young adult leaders who are
at ease with the new developments will be crucial for the Church's
mission. Despite the tragic developments at Sheffield's Nine O'Clock
Service, the Church still needs to take the risk of trusting young leaders
with responsibility to experiment with new forms of worship and discipleship within a clear framework of support and accountability. The
theological foundation of such trust is the Holy Spirit, whose role is to
bring the foretaste of God's future into the present. When the practices of
the past are of limited usefulness, it is the Holy Spirit acting through the
next generation of leaders whom we must trust.

3

Working Spiritually

Send us out in the power of your Spirit
To live and work to your praise and glory.

ASB Rite A Eucharist

3.1   This act of sending out reminds us that our spiritual lives are not meant to be confined to the act of Sunday worship. These words also recall the Great Commission of Matthew 28 as we, like the disciples, seek to live and witness to God's glory in the world (see paragraph 2.34). This does not mean that God is not in the world, but that God's presence may be hidden, distorted, or broken. Christians open to the Holy Spirit have the ability to reclaim for God what is God's in its beauty and grace.

This also means that while spirituality should form the heart of the local church, there will also be other forms of spiritual life among those in the world whom God has already touched; we can discern this and celebrate.

3.2   In this chapter we look at the spiritual lives of young people and consider the task of the Church in nurturing, encouraging and sustaining the relationship young people have with God as part of the Church and also in the world. We also see that the spirituality of young people can add much to the mission dynamic of Matthew 28, as they bring freshness, vitality and new insight to bear on the culture of the Church.

People writing to the report have been quick to say that a person's spirituality is not expressed by passivity, nor is it necessarily expressed by being still, silent and reflective. They have said that spiritual development can take place in loud, noisy places, in rigorous debates, through sport and by watching videos as well as through quiet prayer, meditative services and by appreciation of beautiful places.

It is also important to note that secular youth work has 'spiritual development' among its stated aims. A response from a Local Education Authority highlights 'the need for the Church of England to develop and support the spiritual development curriculum for young people both in the Church and in partnership with a range of agencies, including Local Education Authorities.'

3.3   The development of a spiritual life is an essential part of becoming fully human and the Church has an opportunity of sharing the gospels with young people. The importance of relationships in this spiritual development is crucial.

> Brother John Francis told of his experience with 13/14-year-olds who were not churchgoers but were visiting a local convent.
>
> So I decided to ask them what the words 'Mystery, Wonder and Awe' meant to them. This was their response:
>
> 'Mystery' – 'a Ruth Rendell TV thriller'
>
> 'Wonder' – 'where we're going on holiday'
>
> 'Awe' – 'something they teach us about in school that comes out of the earth'.
>
> Diocesan Youth Officers Conference, 1995

It would be easy to be simplistic about this revelation and to make assumptions about the spiritual life of those who do not come to church; because these young people do not associate spiritual experiences with the words 'awe' and 'wonder' does not mean that these experiences are absent. It is important not to mistake what goes on in our churches as being the same as what goes on within an individual's interior life.

> We have also confused spiritual development and religious development. . . Spiritual development is not about religion. . . It is about getting in touch with the deeper parts of life – valuing the experiences of awe and wonder, of hurt and sorrow, relationships with other people and the natural world, and coming to an understanding of what is meant by the term 'God'.
>
> Francis Cattermole (1990)

3.4   In 'The Religious Experience and Faith Development of Nonchurch-going Young People' (1993), Clapton showed that young people who had little or no experience of the Church were engaged in attempts to create meaning.

> A clear picture has emerged showing the spiritual awareness of non-church young people. They are active in making sense of themselves, the world and the existential questions which they encounter. They are recipients of the most profound religious experiences, comparable with any reported by the church attenders. Finally they make sense of their lives through a faith which is constructed by centres of value and power, creating an 'ultimate environment'.

Such an understanding has implications for the Church, in our pastoral and mission work. Clapton continues:

The process and results of this thesis have profoundly influenced my pastoral work with nonchurch-going young people. I am better informed about the spirituality of such young people, their religious experience and the form these take. As a result of this study I have concluded there is a need to create safe opportunities where young people can speak of their experiences to one another, and arrive at an interpretation with which they are comfortable. In the same way I have now a greater awareness of the construction of young people's faith and how questions and difficulties in life are tackled using varying degrees of development skills. Given this foundation, I am confident that methods can be devised which encourage young people to become aware of and take responsibility for their own faith development.

3.5   The Church has a spiritual heritage, a history, and a wealth of experience of mystery, awe and wonder which is part of its mission to share. This heritage belongs not just to adults but also to young people and children. It also belongs to those outside the Church. How we help each other to engage with this mystery and to encounter God is extremely important, not just for the individuals involved but for the whole Church community. The challenge of working towards active spiritual lives is a challenge which has the power to generate enthusiasm and life and bring deep meanings to our everyday experience (see paragraph 2.16). From Clapton's research it can be seen that many young people naturally have a spiritual dimension to their experience. The Church can work with young people, churched and unchurched, and learn from their own fresh encounters with God. Through them a new and exciting perspective can be brought to the Church.

3.6   Young people can also be deeply committed and sensitive to the struggles of the wider community. It is at this time that a profound affinity can develop for the natural world; the environment and issues such as ecology, care of the world and its resources are crucially important (see paragraph 2.19, section 7). Issues of social justice, politics, and concern for other people are strongly felt and debated. This sensitivity, altruism and commitment is a message from the gospels and is one which young people can help the Church to engage with. Values are not held just by individuals, but also by the community. The Christian community holds Christian values and the Church engages with young people to explore and resource the movement to a better world.

3.7   This chapter explores different ways that young people encounter God, both in their individual lives and in their communities, and how adults are called to walk alongside young people on their spiritual journeys.

Faith development of young people

Adolescence . . . is a time of huge change: physical, mental and emotional. The body changes out of all recognition from its pre-pubescent self and is now ready and willing to explore its sexual identity. The mind develops new ways of thinking and is now able to cope with abstract concepts. Old loyalties and accepted authority structures are now challenged by new relationships outside the family.

Faced with these upheavals, young people find themselves in a position to explore the so-called 'Big Questions' in a new way: 'What am I here for?', 'What's it all about?', 'Who am I?', 'Am I OK?', 'Where am I going?'. These are questions which allow young people to exercise their newly acquired cognitive skills for the first time. For all young people these questions are profoundly theological as they probe into the deepest aspects of faith, and not just religious faith.

Daniel Tyndall (1995)

3.8   The changes of adolescence often produce inner turmoil within individuals and this can leave adults feeling inadequate and unsure of how best to help. The Church has a pastoral responsibility for people going through times of rapid change; it also has a heritage of understanding how creative these times of personal and spiritual growth can be. This time of searching is crucial for young people and if the Church is able and willing to engage with them in the search, it too can be creatively renewed, tested and refined better to fulfil its mission of witnessing to Jesus Christ in today's world.

Faith development theory

3.9   Faith development theory aims to tease out significant trends or phases which many people follow in their spiritual journeys. Although people are individuals, there are certain general patterns and stages which most pass through. To use the language and scheme of James Fowler (1981), the majority of teenagers are in stage 3 (explained below), while most of the 21–30 age group are in transition to stage 4.

Stage 3 (Fowler's stage of 'synthetic-conventional faith') may be described as a stage of conforming faith. It is often entered around age twelve. The ability to think abstractly has now developed and, by comparison with earlier stages, there is a new capacity for mutual, interpersonal perspective-taking. What peers, parents, teachers (and sometimes church leaders) say is particularly important at this stage, and personal relationships are highly significant. This is, therefore, a time of going with a particular 'faith-current' or 'faith-crowd'.

Those who are at this stage are sometimes said to be 'embedded' in their faith outlook; they are not yet able to reflect on their beliefs and values. Thus, although the circle of people we relate to at this stage does so much to provide our meaning-making we are largely unaware of this process . . . Perhaps this partly explains the notorious difficulty of reasoning with young people about the views they hold and the influences that others hold over them.

The transition to Faith Stage 4 , which itself may take several years, is often entered into at around 17 or 18 years old . . . It involves a psychological – and often literal – 'leaving home': a distancing from others who have been so significant to me before, as I leap out of the faith-current and discover who I am and what I really believe for myself. Stage 4 (Fowler's stage of 'individuative-reflective' faith) may thus be described as the stage of choosing faith. It is marked by a double development . . .

I am now able to take a 'third person' perspective, a 'transcending stand-point' from which I can evaluate my beliefs and relationships. In this stage I can no longer tolerate having my faith at second-hand: I must know who I am for myself, when I am not being defined by my rela-tionships with other people. Beliefs and commitments which previously were rather unexamined can now be consciously adopted; faith can become one's own. The transition to this stage of faith can be long and traumatic.

Christian ministers and educators need to be particularly sensitive here, allowing young people space to grow out of one stage of 'faithing' to another. For many this will seem to be a loss of faith, but it is in fact only a loss of one way of being in faith in order to take a very different way.

Jeff Astley (1995)

John Finney also notes:

There was general agreement that the majority of children drift away from the Church in their early teens. The Church has a poor image amongst the youth, and cannot compete with conflicting interests. Leaving it also represents a form of rebellion against authority.

Finding Faith Today (1992) p.13

3.10   Jeff Astley also links identity formation and the conversion experience. He cites Erik Erikson (1958), who writes that when individuals are in an identity crisis they need devotion to a meaningful trustable reality in which they can rest their hearts. For many, this leads to a profound longing for, and turning to God.

Faith development theory, however, only provides a 'context' into which the Gospel may be proclaimed. The conversion experience and the manner of knowing the saving power of God described in Ephesians 2 is not automatically a result of faith development. What faith development theory gives us is an insight into the contexts of young people's spiritual development, such that the most sensitive and appropriate methods of speaking about the Gospel and sharing faith may be used.

3.11   Knowing that young people are experiencing these sorts of thoughts and feelings can help improve our sensitivity and ability to walk alongside them. Some of the work that the Church is doing documented in this report is certainly providing faith-currents, and faith-crowds, in which young people can come to know God. Other pieces of work which are going on in the Church are geared more to personal reflection and incorporate an understanding and acceptance that young people want to experience their faith 'first hand'. Work that springs from both developmental stages is dependent on the way adults respond and are prepared to engage with the young people.

> The nurturing role of the mentor in encouraging the move to adult 'faithing', from second-hand to first-hand, may be crucial at this time. There is some evidence that 'faith models', who possess such a sense of identity themselves and who remain faithful to their own visions, are of great importance to young people in their transition to Stage 4.
>
> Jeff Astley (1995)

Encounters of young people with God

> Often when I am walking down a road and I can see other people walking too, either in the same direction as me or in the other direction, I feel we are all part of something much larger which we can't really explain, but which we can be aware of. Often too I feel a presence with me, it can comfort me when I am worried about something or when things seem to be going right for me, it seems to fill me with an amazing sense of happiness, completeness and knowledge that everything is somehow in control. Being a Christian I would call this God.
>
> Edward Robinson and Michael Jackson (1987) p.20

Keeping going and growing as a Christian in my life has not always been easy and has had many ups and downs. To try and help myself I try each day to read and study God's word, the Bible as well as pray to Him, placing all I am doing and going to do in his hands. I also attend Church and my university Christian Union both of which have provided me with much encouragement and support. My family have aided my growth as a Christian, and increasingly so as I have been willing to share both the joys and trials with them. Keeping going is hard work – but worth it.

Kesia, aged 20, testimony to the Working Party

3.12   In the 1995 Diocesan Youth Officers' Conference entitled 'Mystery, Awe and Wonder' (see paragraphs 3.3 and 2.26), the youth officers explored and shared ways in which these encounters occur. There was a feeling that creating opportunities by building in reflective times within a programme was a good way of ministering to young people. The question of balance and giving young people choice was crucial in terms of a good programme. To ignore opportunities to share spiritual stories was felt to be as unhelpful as producing contrived emotional experiences.

Responses from all over the country show that it is apparent that many youth workers aware of the importance of spirituality to young people are engaged with them in exploring their religious lives.

Within the community

3.13   Young people have opportunities to develop their faith both through individual searching and by a range of opportunities which they can develop and take part in, provided by others in the Church. Although the activities below are innovative and challenging many people have written and expressed concern at how limited the resources are for this work. Much of the work takes place by extremely committed and caring individuals who are seriously concerned about young people within the Church. Many of these people are young themselves. Given more acknowledgement, encouragement, support and physical resources the enthusiasm and excellent work shown below could flourish and really reach many more young people.

Worship in church

3.14   Many people look for church worship to provide them with a spiritual energy to equip them for the following week. If this is to be available for young people then they need to be asked how the worship can be spiritually invigorating for them. In the same way that there is not just one way that adults like to worship, there is not a single prescriptive service that young people would adopt wholeheartedly. (see paragraph 4.2). By working with young people, churches or communities have found a range of different ways of worshipping which are helpful. In some dioceses there are interesting examples of small groups of young people who are taking initiatives within worship to broaden services in the church.

> The Hit Squad is a group of young people, aged 18 and upwards, working in the Carlisle Diocese with the aim of helping to introduce new ideas into regular worship. The group visit a parish for a weekend, during which time they work with young people of the parish to devise and organise the Sunday morning worship. Using the framework of the ASB service still leaves scope for the use of drama, dance and music as well as a 'talkie' slot and prayers.

> Once the Squad is approached by an interested parish a contact is formed between the vicar and the nearest Hit Squad member. This member would then make a 'pre-Hit' visit to establish a link with the parish and to finalise details regarding the service, preparation, time and accommodation. The theme for the service can either be picked by the parish or by the Squad, and does not necessarily have to follow the set theme in the lectionary.

> By providing this facility the group hopes to help parishes by showing them that services do not always have to be straight ASB, but can have a bit of variety which will interest people from 3 to 93.

3.15   Young people are often thirsting for worship and meaning, even though this may not be the experience of a harassed youth worker struggling with the 'God–slot' as part of their programme. A candle lit at the end of a busy session can profoundly reach a group of young people as a space becomes available for reflection, thanksgiving and intercession. However, this only works if it is part of the whole ethos of the group. Worship which is integrated and part of the lives of young people, which springs from their own experience and which they are part of, is much more likely to be useful and welcomed by the group.

Christian organisations

3.16   There are many organisations working in England which attract large numbers of young people. Some of these organisations work very closely with churches.

> The Church Pastoral Aid Society (CPAS) has a large number of church based groups throughout England. There are Pathfinders for

young people aged between 11 and 14 years and Church Youth Fellowship Association (CYFA) groups for 14- 18-year-olds.

The CPAS provides:

* resources – teaching materials to help leaders teach the Bible to group members

* regular mailings – to all group leaders to train them and encourage them in their youth work and to provide news and information

* training – at local, regional and national level, specific to their situation and age group and emphasising the church-based nature of the work

* membership – of a large national and (with groups in Europe) international organisation providing links with other group members and members events

* CYFA Pathfinder staff – to do the theological thinking about youth work which local leaders have little time to do and therefore provide a theological base for the work

The CPAS offer residential opportunities for young people through their CYFA/Pathfinder ventures which incorporates Falcon Holidays for disadvantaged young people who would not otherwise get a holiday. Staffed by over 750 volunteers in 1994, 5,306 young people of secondary age participated in these residential programmes taking place in 45 venues throughout the country.

Girls' Friendly Society

The GFS was started in 1875 with a purpose to rescue the most vulnerable from the evils of the time. Our work is still in great demand, and many of the problems still exist. The Society now campaigns under the name of Platform For Young Women.

The Girls' Friendly Society is a place for young women to receive support, make new friends, discover talents and encounter God. Their experience may be in the parish branch, housing scheme, community project or in the worldwide family of GFS.

Within the capacity of our resources we try to offer vulnerable young women a platform and a firm foundation: a new start, a fresh opportunity to face the future with confidence and to take control of their lives. We provide 350 bed spaces and we also offer support and advice. Within the housing schemes and other projects we help young women to care for themselves and to begin to fulfil their potential.

3.17   Many other organisations operate nationally. Some, like the Mothers' Union, have a membership which includes those under twenty-five and work hard to ensure that they are attractive to the younger group.

The United Society for the Propagation of the Gospel (USPG) have 'root groups' for those between 18 and 30 and also have an exchange scheme where young people can spend some time abroad. Scripture Union and Youth for Christ provide resources, publish a magazine and run events over England, as do the Church Missionary Society (CMS).

Special events and festivals

3.18   Many projects, youth clubs and churches put on, or attend special events in addition to their normal programme. These range from inviting a group such as the Hit Squad, Holy Disorder or similar team, into the area, to putting on a large celebration or festival (see paragraph 4.17). They can run for an evening, or a day, or can be residential.

> Greenbelt is unique. It is an arts festival designed to celebrate the creativity in all of us which comes from being made by God. It takes place in the Northamptonshire countryside over the four day bank holiday weekend at the end of August.
>
> Contributors are drawn from around the globe to play their part in an unequalled programme of music, drama, dance, literature, fine art, craft, film and fashion; together with incisive seminars on the kind of issues which matter most. The objective is to stretch the hearts and minds of all who come and send them back home to tackle the delights and rigours of God's world with a renewed and informed sense of urgency.
>
> We believe firmly that Jesus Christ is involved in all creation and that in his world there is no division between sacred and secular. As a result, personal faith, doubt, politics, social concern, mission, ethics, creativity, work and play are all addressed with seriousness and hilarity in equal parts. Individuals are inspired with a sense of freedom and opportunities as followers of Christ beyond the narrow confines of conventional piety.
>
> Reverence and the lack of it are parallel features of the Greenbelt Festival as up to 25,000 participants worship, learn and argue together.
>
> Greenbelt is not fundamentally a youth event, though roughly two thirds of those who come are between the ages of 15 and 30.
>
> Leaflet from Greenbelt promoting their work

The Loweswater Youth Festival, Cumbria:

In 1994 the parish organised its fifth annual youth festival which attracted 60 teenagers and 16 leaders. As its reputation grows, teenagers are coming from further afield. Organising special events like this is a way to attract young people to the church. The vicar of Loweswater works with local talented leaders to put together the twelve hour day – 10 am to 10 pm – packed with workshops on banners and kites, screen printing, printing T-shirts, folk music and dance. There are also activities such as raft-making, rowing boats, canoeing, drama, dry stone walling, mountain rescue expedition, ghyll-climbing and a gentle ecology walk.

The event is achieved through excellent local co-operation and prior organisation. The local mountain rescue team helps and the nearby management training centre provides instructors. The County Youth Service supplies the minibus, Canadian canoes and a further instructor. The diocesan youth officer helped and no fewer than 25 people provided cakes to feed the young people throughout the day, with shepherd's pie for all coming from nine local farmhouses.

Worship is at 5.30 pm which is followed by supper and folk dancing.

3.19   Many of these special events help young people to explore and promote their gifts and talents. There may be musical, artistic, literary, dramatic or circus skills workshops, which can then be put together in a celebration as the climax of the event. Alternatively there may be quieter or more reflective outcomes as different ideas are explored throughout the day.

Music and Worship Workshop Days, Diocese of York

The purpose of the first day was to 'offer enjoyable and practical ways of exploring music and worship' and this attracted about 150 participants from 11 to 70 from virtually every denomination. They enjoyed workshops in leading worship with guitar; organ playing (advanced and basic); worship teams; Taizé music; audio equipment in churches; arranging music for instruments; and 'Sing to the Lord a New Song'. Young people were especially encouraged to attend and following the success of this day other days have been arranged at diocesan and deanery level.

The time of the year determines theme and content to a great extent. A February day prepares for Lent and Easter, while a November day prepares for Advent, Christmas and Epiphany. Themes are held to lightly with such a large ecumenical gathering. The emphasis is on exploring, sharing and gaining insight and expertise. The format of the day has always been the same and seems to work very well indeed with a chance to go to two workshops. An introductory talk sets the tone for the day, uniting and inspiring people, and offering thoughts on music in worship in today's churches. On two of our days John Bell of the Iona Community has given the lead with tremendous enthusiasm.

Residentials

3.20   Residentials provide the opportunity for young people to spend time together and live away from their normal environment. The range of activities and experiences which can be fitted into an extended programme, sometimes in beautiful surroundings, means that these times away often profoundly affect young people. The residential also gives a chance for the young people to live in 'community', albeit a temporary one, and to learn from one another, laying the foundations for future work when the group returns home.

There is almost an infinite number of different types of residentials which can be run to provide different challenges and opportunities to different groups.

A recent mailing from the Diocese of Chelmsford included information about the following residentials:

Small Groups weekend – an activity weekend where small groups can join together in a full programme of sports, games, worship and social activities held in a centre.

The South Downs Way – a camping and walking weekend expedition.

A week with the community at Taizé in France- to share in all the prayer, the discussions, the meals, the walks, the silence, the singing, and the gatherings at Oyak.

Summer Activity Break – 3 days where individual young people can take part in indoor and outdoor activities, games and workshops, plan worship and make new friends.

Confirmation weekend – for young people preparing for confirmation or recently confirmed, activities, worship and reflection.

'What shall I do with my life?' – a weekend offering time and opportunity to reflect on their vocations.

3.21　Some residentials are planned at parish, deanery or diocesan level, 'from scratch' with the group and their leaders organising all aspects of the time away. However, increasing use is being made of residential centres which are equipped and prepared to greet groups and have facilities and expert leadership to enable a full and exciting programme. The examples below show two such centres.

Champion House, in the beautiful Edale valley of the Peak District, is the diocesan youth house for the Diocese of Derby. It is run by the Warden who is also the Vicar of Edale village which allows the house to be linked closely with the community in which it is set.

The original house was a converted barn which has been carefully extended so that the house can be run as two separate self-catering units or as a single. The accommodation is in small dormitory rooms with bunk beds.

The house is used in a variety of ways. Parish groups, both from the diocese and beyond, come with their young people and run individual programmes on, for example, building group cohesion, pre-confirmation, etc. Groups of parishes or deaneries which have fewer young people join to make a larger group. There are several diocesan weekends during a year, for example, on youth leader training, spirituality, post-confirmation and for young people from clergy families. Mid-week bookings are usually from schools and other youth organisations.

This is a good example of a diocese supporting a building (and all that goes with it) to promote work with young people. It has the advantage of a purpose built building, a skilled Warden and co-operation with the diocesan youth office, as well as local conditions ideal for climbing, walking and other outdoor pursuits.

For non-church groups using the building, certain furnishings proclaim it a Christian house and the hope is that the way in which it deals with people is also proclaims the interest of the Church in all young people.

The Warden adds:
Residential centres are quietly getting on with a huge amount of youth work which largely remains unrecognised.

Champion House hosts 144,000 working hours for young people each year (assuming eight hours sleep which doesn't always happen!). The Church of England alone has seventeen centres. An estimate of the number of working youth hours provided by the

Residential Centre Wardens Network Centres is 1,632,00 hours per year.

Crathorne Campsite – a resource in York Diocese
Crathorne Campsite is a small camping facility for youth groups, in the grounds of an ancient rectory. The campsite began twenty years ago with a loo-block built by local young people on a government training scheme . The campsite now has a well equipped, self catering kitchen and a supply of tents and marquees. The site is registered with the environmental health department of the council.

The campsite has been mainly self-funded though grants from Children in Need, Telethon, Stokesley Deanery and York Diocese have bought equipment and allowed some poorly resourced inner city groups to use the camp free of charge.

Each year the campsite caters for about twenty-five non-uniformed and uniformed groups, some 400 young people in all.

The ethos of the site is 'small is beautiful' and does show what might be done with a limited but very useful space and a little imagination.

3.22   There are many innovative residential opportunities for young people. Many groups have exchange visits with young people from over-seas. The Diocese of Liverpool is working with Nigeria and the Czech Republic. The Diocese of Exeter worked in 1995 on exchange visits with South Africa. One particularly exciting project involved young people from an Urban Priority Area in East London flying to Kenya and working with the community to help to establish good water supplies (see paragraph 4.31).

Camps and holidays
3.23   Some organisations have a full programme of Christian holidays, breaks or festivals. The age range is large and the organisation and expec-tations from these events can be quite different.

Crusaders
Crusaders offer a large range of holidays in this country and abroad. Their aims include being exciting, Christian-based, safe and value for money. Holidays offer activities, sports, excursions, relaxation. These are part of the wider mission of Crusaders whose aim is to 'help today's young people get to know Jesus Christ'. The object is to prepare these youngsters (8-18 years) for responsible Christian living in tomorrow's world and to develop their gifts of leadership. The holi-days build on the work of over 400 groups across England, Scotland and Wales with over 18,000 young people attending.

Morning Star Trust

This is a Christian charitable organisation which since 1981 has been running off-shore sailing activities and sail-training courses. They aim to help young people gain in confidence; overcome fears; discover and develop their gifts as individuals; and learn their value as members of a team. Two sailing vessels are based on the River Medway and sail along the East coast and out across the North Sea to Belgium, Holland and France. The Morning Star team members are motivated by their commitment to Jesus Christ, share their faith where it is welcomed and appropriate, and aim to encourage and build up everyone who sails with them regardless of ethnic or cultural background.

Retreats

3.24   Retreats give an opportunity of drawing away from the immediate demands of everyday life and dwelling on the deeper spiritual aspects of oneself or the community. For young people a retreat can be crucial in helping to locate God's calling and discover how to respond to it.

A weekend on the Northumberland coast exploring Celtic spirituality

The Celtic Christians believed in a world where God was within the work and experiences of everyday life. In today's pressurised world, starved of the spiritual, many are turning again to the art, music and prayers of the Celts for their earthy imagery and glimpse of connectedness. Over the weekend we will be introduced to the culture and spirituality of the Celts – with illustrated talks and workshops. We spend Saturday visiting the island of Lindisfarn and the birthplace of Celtic Christianity in England.

SCM Conferences

Pilgrimage

3.25   Many young people discover deep spiritual meaning through pilgrimage. The act of travelling on a 'holy quest' provides time of reflection and an opportunity to dwell on the spiritual journey that the person is engaged in. Also, there is much to be gained from visiting sites which have been significant to our spiritual ancestors or are places which have been steeped in worship and prayer for many years.

My parish of St Faith's, North Dulwich (Southwark Diocese) has been involved in young people's pilgrimages for a period of eight years. A number of like-minded parishes in the Anglican Catholic tradition joined together in the Southwark Churches Pilgrimage to the Shrine of Our Lady of Walsingham.

There was a challenge being given to these youngsters even for these days of imaginative school trips. Our kids did not misbehave because there was a task to be achieved, to walk to each night's destination which we invariably limped into – sharing our experiences of blistered feet.

And of course we prayed together which meant so much more because of our shared experience. Each day before setting off there was a Mass. I believe that Catholic spirituality especially emphasises the incarnation. For our group of twenty this translated into saying Mass within the intimacy of the crowded hall in which we had spent the previous night.

We sat round in our sleeping bags. The wine was passed round in the mugs we were using, the bread was of the loaves we were carrying with us. This was the 'transcendent' right in the middle of our 'here and now' experience of the youth walk. I know this has remained very important to the young people who took part.

3.26   Some young people also make pilgrimages to sites which are significant in terms of what is happening there now. A community which is extremely popular with young people is Taizé. The Archbishop of Canterbury led a large group of a thousand young people from churches from all the dioceses of England on a pilgrimage to Taizé in 1992.

Comments from young people attending the Archbishop's pilgrimage

Every person in Taizé is treated as an equal. You can be in church for 5 minutes or 5 hours and no one doubts your faith.

Jessica Mannes, Chelmsford

Everyone in Taizé is trusted and respected for who they are.

Simon, Canterbury

We are so proud of our Christian faith and charged by our experience on pilgrimage to Taizé that we implore you to help us to help other young people meet God through the simplicity of the liturgy, through silent periods for meditation, reflection and conversation with God through the truth of our faith.

Jane Carnell and Katie Dane, Canterbury

At Taizé I could feel the real strength and love of God.

Tracy Woolard, St Edmundsbury and Ipswich

Taizé was the unique experience I needed to confirm my doubts and discover what really mattered.

Nicola, Chelmsford

Responsibility for others. Loving them and being with them and keep on being with them.

Sam Brown, Southwell

Taizé strengthens your faith in Christ and makes faith grow and grow.

Jennifer, Canterbury

Taizé

It couldn't be simpler, it couldn't be clearer, it was this simple truth. God has nothing to give but his love. The message from Taizé was about uncovering, re-discovering the wellsprings of our faith and that is just what happened to a typical bunch of pilgrims from the Durham Diocese who spent a July week in Taizé, the Miracle Monastery of Burgundy founded by Brother Roger in 1945 and a centre of pilgrimage for thousands upon thousands. Most were under 30, one was 70. Sixteen year olds were seen going to church half an hour before the service to enjoy the music and the peace; others stayed on till midnight in the candlelight till long after the Community music had ended and a few solo voices took up Taizé chants in turn.

We met fellow pilgrims from twenty other countries in the marquee at meal times, in worship at the bar, in the bazaar and in the loos. Even though there were 3,000 fellow campers Taizé always had space, space for one another and space for God.

Annual Report of Church Lads' and Church Girls' Brigade

Education

3.27   The Church has a considerable role and influence within all aspects of formal education in England. Many people who work in schools and colleges have deep personal faiths and teach or lecture in the secular world. It is important that these callings are recognised, supported and appreciated by the Church as being as significant as callings to church-based ministry. The influence of individual Christians working in either state schools and colleges or Church institutions is considerable.

Schools

3.28   There are good links between churches and some schools, which have working partnerships with organisations which run assemblies and contribute to the religious curriculum in the schools. However sometimes unhelpful stereotypes exist, which disadvantage joint working.

All too often, 'youth' and 'schools' or 'colleges' have cartoon images of each other and keep a distance. Where this happens great opportunities are missed.

The truth is that a significant number of teachers and lecturers are Christians and have the instincts of youth workers and work with young people outside the formal curriculum.

Virtually all the young people of the locality are assembled at the school and a large number in the college. These institutions offer a good channel of communication and publicity for youth initiatives and a good point of contact for youth workers.

There is an overlap of curriculum between the two sectors: in addition to religious and spiritual dimensions, there is a joint concern for health and sex education; personal/social/moral education, outdoor pursuits, politics, residential field trips, to name but a few. Often resources and training share common elements. Some schools and colleges are most creative about liturgy.

Some excellent projects come from a community partnership between youth workers and schools, for example: the young pilgrimage, the all night vigil, the dramatic performance in Holy Week, the forum on knotty issues, the campaign for a greater justice and a better environment. . .

When 'youth' and 'schools' or 'colleges' combine their young talents and their adult talents wide and strong youth work can result.

Tristam Jenkins, Director of Education, Diocese of Hereford

3.29   The potential for joint or shared working is enormous. Some Christian projects work very closely with schools and these partnerships can be very useful in building relationships with young people who have no contact with the gospel. Many Christian residential centres are working flexibly from the schools' agenda to open access to their buildings and offer visits which meet core elements of the national curriculum.

The Diocese of Worcester has a residential centre called The Far Forest Centre which is available for all sorts of groups of young people to use. This facility gives the opportunity for links and partnerships between the diocese and other organisations. This shared working can be shown by the following: 'we offer a free photocopiable village study pack to small groups which provides National Curriculum resource material for Key Stage 2 pupils'.

3.30   The Church also has many maintained schools in England which are supported by the National Society. They also publish a range of resources which support the Church's work with schools.

There are 807,000 pupils in the maintained schools in England which have a Church of England foundation (Aided, Controlled, Special Agreement or Grant Maintained). Of these 57,000 are in the age range 14-17 and a small number are in the 18-21 age range. About half of these pupils are girls and half are boys.

In the private sector 62,000 pupils between the age of 14-17 are at schools with an Anglican chaplain; of these about a quarter are girls and three quarters are boys.

David Lankshear, The National Society, January 1995

Further education sector

Further education (FE) is arguably the most diverse and challenging sector of education for the Churches' youth, not least because such large numbers of the population have links and associations with their local FE and sixth form colleges (465 in England). There are 377,000 students aged 14-17; 754,000 aged 18-21; and 372,000 aged 22–5 in institutions in FE in the United Kingdom. Here, on the doorsteps of churches, are many opportunities to meet a generation almost entirely ignorant of the Church and alienated from organised religion. Chaplaincy is perhaps the most visible aspect of the Church's involvement in FE. There are 230 FE chaplains in England, of whom 134 are Anglican, there is a significant growth in the number of full-time appointments with strong links with the parishes and ecumenical bodies. Another aspect of the Church's engagement with young people is through the promotion of spiritual, moral and personal values in the FE curriculum.

FE sector colleges are keen to expand their appointment of full-time detached youth workers. Evidence from the National Youth Agency indicates there are at least 50 who have attended their 1994 training conference.

David Lankshear, The National Society, January 1995

3.31   There are key areas, where Christians can express their faith identified by the Joint National Adviser in Further Education, Revd Clifford Jenkins.

Programmes of study have to take account of ethical and moral considerations. Those who design study programmes will ensure that Christian values are reflected within the curriculum.

Pastoral work in colleges tends to be led by secular counsellors, but the example of Jesus Christ in his encounter with people serves as a model for Christians to be involved as tutors, course leaders or as members of the administrative or domestic staff.

Christian groups of various kinds exist in many colleges where Christian students and staff can explore the relationship of their faith to the modern world and encourage and affirm each other's faith.

Worship is not a legal requirement in colleges of further education. However, staff and students can arrange special services, e.g. memorial or carol services.

Chaplains are being appointed to further education colleges in increasing numbers. They can provide pastoral support, work with students and staff to plan acts of worship, support Christian groups and help Christians and members of other faiths to build bridges between the local worshipping community and the college.

Locally some churches have been building up good working relationships with their local colleges and these partnerships and opportunities to work together are important.

Higher education

3.32   There has been an enormous expansion in higher education in the last five years. Far more young people are experiencing it, and financial support for students has changed drastically. Debt is now normal and is an issue for pastoral concern. Churches need to be aware of the changed and changing student experience. Parents and church members might mistakenly assume student life to be like theirs. This is not the case. Many students have to take part-time, badly paid work to make ends meet, this affects time for study and time for leisure. There is no time to go to church or to be part of the community in student clubs and activities. 'If the Church doesn't join in the changes in education it will no longer be part of the solution' Paul Brice, National Officer for Higher Education for the Church of England.

> *There are 533,000 students aged 18–21 and 208,000 aged 21–25 in higher education in the United Kingdom who are also resident in the United Kingdom. There are 129 full time and 50 part-time Anglican chaplains in higher education institutes in England. There*

are twelve Anglican colleges of higher education in England, and 33,000 full time undergraduate students attending these colleges.

David Lankshear, The National Society, January 1995

The changing face of education means that students are more like customers who can pick and choose and make demands, and colleges are responding to this with greater flexibility.

The danger for the Church is that someone coming in assuming their experience of education is normal will find most churches patronising and rigid in how they offer Christian education.

The Church might find itself losing members and not realise why. It is increasingly important therefore to listen to members, and outsiders, so as to know what is demanded of it. We have not been very good at that in the past. Now we must try to listen more and at the same time start listening to children and youth.

Paul Brice, National Officer for Higher Education, Church of England

Expectations in education

3.33   It is apparent that education, and the experience of growing up today is not the same as someone now in their forties or fifties remembers it. A young person nowadays is far more likely to enter into continuing education, this by and large is a greater commitment than for a student twenty years ago. There are financial implications which mean many young people have to work to get through college, and increased expectations on achieving academic qualifications which mean greater time is spent working. Consequently time for a religious dimension to life is squeezed out by other pressures and regular church attendance is very difficult to maintain. The Church can find ways to 'fit in' to these new lifestyles. A weekend retreat which has space, teaching and recreation is more likely to be accommodated than a regular service once a week. When a person makes time to spend a weekend away, it has to be good. The expectations of young people are based on their experience of a sophisticated education system, the media and being part of an information age. Although an event does not have to be 'high tech' it does have to have a quality and be well thought out if it is to be seen as valid and worth spending time on.

Within this context, there is an amazing amount of work going on throughout England which is often on a shoestring budget. Problems with finance in some dioceses mean that even the limited resources that are spent on these ventures may be under threat. A diocesan youth officer writes 'Parish funding is quietly being reduced in response to the Commissioners problems. Residentials for example are not being funded by parish councils who would have been generous in the past'. It is not enough to value this excellent work; it needs to be resourced to continue and grow.

Personal journeys

Spiritual guidance

> When I started going to church I was very excited about the whole thing, you know, God, prayer, everything. I didn't want anything special, I just wanted to talk about it, but there didn't seem any room to do this. The vicar was busy, everyone was busy, and there didn't seem any space to talk about God. I wanted to know if the people in church prayed at home. If they did, how did they do it? I wanted to know so much, and to talk about how it felt for me. It was ages like this, and church felt a bit empty and apart from my own attempts to pray and things.

> It was Joyce who noticed me, she gave me a beautiful card and understood that I was doing something valuable and special in trying to pray. Even though I was young and she was old we were doing the same thing.
>
> Member of a congregation, Diocese of St Albans

3.34 Almost everyone who has a spiritual life can look back and see important people who have pointed out a road ahead and supported them on their journey. Adults are often surprised to realise that they may be such models for young people. Many adults feel that they are not good enough for this work and are very uncomfortable at the thought of their own struggling religious life being a model for anyone. As one diocesan officer wrote 'What adults are desperately afraid of is that they will be questioned and challenged about their faith'. Although this reticence is understandable, if adults fail to share the experience that they have then young people are left alone to work it out by themselves. Young people will then lack that personal support through relationship which is so important in a faith journey.

John Lee, former diocesan youth officer for Bath and Wells, has published a small book on spiritual development. In it he gives four 'rules of the road' which encourage the youth worker to respect every young person as human; to see spiritual development as the underlying curriculum for all work; to see the youth worker as the primary resource for spiritual development; and not to separate people into 'religious' and 'non-religious'. John goes on to suggest ten skills that are useful for youth workers and to give very practical advice on bringing spiritual development to the heart of work with young people. This work is varied, active and not 'typically spiritual'. Although there is a space for quiet and reflection, this is not the only 'spiritual' time.

✗ John sees spiritual development taking place in every piece of youth work and sees it as a living process enmeshed in relationships and lubricated with humour. He ends his book thus 'Here is one way to tell if your spiritual development is at an end: if you are still alive – then it isn't over!'

This need to provide many experiences within relationships is echoed by Jeff Astley in his paper to the Working Party.

> *Active involvement in, and experience of, challenging experiences and a variety of cultures may also be necessary if adolescents are to develop so as to take on the serious burden of responsibility for their own beliefs and commitments. We should recognise that 'the transition from a conformist faith to a mature, self-owned faith may be a rocky road, strewn with spiritual doubts and questions. Some never risk it.*

> Jeff Astley (1995)

Exploring a calling

3.35 Young people are spiritual people and have a place in the spiritual life of the Church; they are called by God in many different ways. They welcome a range of activities and opportunities which extend, nurture and promote their faith and help them to explore the very best ways to lead their lives. They live in a world of many meanings and the Church has an opportunity to share a theology which gives meaning and direction in a seemingly confused and chaotic world. Youth work is concerned with personal development, Christian youth work sees Christ as the model of personal development and seeks to share this (see paragraphs 2.21–3). Young people wrestle not only with their own identity but with existential questions. This reflection and struggle for deeper meanings is not just an individual endeavour but takes place within groups and in the community. It is also linked to passionate care and concern for the environment, justice and peace. The energy from such concern can help the Church to be rooted in essential matters and remain grounded in the crucial mission of the Church of bringing the gospels to a rapidly changing and restless world.

> *We need to restore the place of spirituality in the public as well as in the private world; relating it to truth as well as to personal experience. It should be understood as the essential source of character development for a society based on sacrificial love.*

> Paragraph 2.19, section 4

3.36   The way individuals in the Church address this mission is varied, imaginative and commendable. However, there is a real concern about how high a priority this work is in the Church. Often the budgets to support youth workers, diocesan youth officers, youth projects or work by individual parishes are extremely small. Work with young people often reflects the experience of the adult twenty years ago and does not encompass the enormous changes in education and information availability. The relationship and partnerships with schools, further education colleges and higher education institutes is inordinately valuable in maintaining contact with a huge number of young people who never come to church.

3.37   The Church has a vital role in working with young people, providing them with opportunities to discover their callings, to explore their spirituality and to share with them the message of the gospels. For this to be most effective the ways of working must start with where young people are, and with what they want. Work that springs from this has great potential in bringing life to the Church and refreshing the spiritual heart of Christianity in England.

4

Young People's Space

4.1   Young people are a vital part of the Church. However, they are marginalised and their contributions to worship and policy making are peripheral. This chapter looks at the place of young people in worship, parish life and in the Church structures. There are comments on the limitations that young people encounter, and the frustrations that they find. There are also examples of work going on both in and outside the Church which enable young people to encounter God and to work to enrich their churches and congregations. The work of the Church is seen holistically not only in the work within it but also in the context of the work of the gospel in the world (see paragraph 2.5).

Worship

> Worship for young people often means that a guitar is wheeled in and a modern hymn is sung. Worship by young people means that you have to have a drama bit.
>
> Young person's comment on youth worship

4.2   This caricature of worship for young people is held by many well-meaning people. Using a guitar in the service often represents a huge stride by the congregation to welcome young people into the service. However, for the young people it may not be enough, and can be seen as a rather patronising gesture. In churches of different traditions the gesture may be different but may leave the young people feeling the same. The gulf between what the church expects and what is comfortable for young people can be enormous (see paragraph 2.11).

4.3   A concern many young people have is not that the service feels strange, but that the older people who run the church expect the young people to fit in and become miniature clones of themselves. For the older people to share their spirituality and their worship as equals would be welcomed by many young people. The difficulties and division occur when young people are expected to assent to others' viewpoints and ideologies without question (see paragraph 2.7).

The liturgy and the style of worship can also exclude young people. A diocesan youth officer comments that what is wanted is 'liturgy that is youth friendly – forms of prayer and praise that are authorised by canon.' He also asks for 'youth awareness and the ability to be able to participate in, rather than be an observer of, worship.'

4.4   The Church has to be prepared to ask young people how they feel about worship and to engage in a real dialogue with openness and with a willingness to try new things and to change. Many young people are equipped by modern education to negotiate and argue their points con-structively and are often willing to try to understand the feelings of older members of the congregation. Others feel alienated from the education system and, while sometimes unable to articulate their points of view, feel passionately and deeply about their faith. It is when young people feel that they have no voice and are impotent that feelings of frustration can turn to anger and disappointment with the result that they leave the Church.

Spirituality

4.5   Having a sense of 'other', an inner identity, which may be seen as a perception of 'God', is a universal human experience (see paragraph 2.24). Every society has some sort of organisation which reflects this. Theologians who have researched 'faith development' have identified stages through which people pass as they come to understand, value and interpret that which they take to be the ultimate. The Church, which has a tradition and a history of encouraging people in their spiritual growth, has an opportunity to share profoundly with young people and to support and nurture them in their faith journeys. If this sharing takes place in dialogue, the Church will be challenged and itself refined by the experience: (see chapter 3 and paragraph 2.8). This sharing is a two-way experience: both the young person and the Church can benefit from using this time cre-atively. The Church has a pastoral duty to these young people and it can offer help and support during times of spiritual growth. The energy that is present when teenagers profoundly and enthusiastically seek God and respond to this deep calling is an energy which is vital to the Church. We suggest that young people's spirituality is explored in dialogue and in a climate of mutual learning and respect. In this way young people can work with others in the Church with a common purpose and mission.

Traditional roles of young people within worship

4.6   Young people have many traditional roles within the worshipping community. In many churches, young people lead worship in the choir, as bell ringers and as servers.

Serving, if done properly, is a discipline of the service of God at the altar and a deepening of the server's own spiritual relationship with, and awareness of, God. The server is trained in this ritual of the altar which, although there might be individual parish variations, is basically the same throughout the world. The server should also be made aware that he/she has the responsibility of making their own preparation before Mass, as well as the opportunity of worshipping God in prayer and service.

Servers work as a team and there should be fellowship amongst them.

Vicar in the Diocese of London

4.7 In other churches young people steward and take the collection. These roles are seen by those young people and the churches as being important: a way in which they can contribute and have their own status, responsibilities and entitlements. Bishop Lindsay Urwin says that through the young people's ministry the hope is to 'engender a love for the Church, the institutional Church, and to help them see that it has got great possibilities for them'. In the best use of these offices young people fulfil necessary functions in the running of their churches and are integral and vital to the worship (see appendix for list of functions and duties).

Bell Ringers

There are 9,693 young people (10–25 years) that serve as bell ringers in the Church of England. Nearly four thousand of these are between the ages of 14 and 17. One in every four bell ringers is under twenty five.

Servers

There are 20,835 young people who are servers. The peak age range is between 14 and 17 with 9,444 young people working as servers.

Choir

There are 28,355 young people who are active members of a choir. The most popular age for choir membership is 10-13 years. Approximately one in every three choir members is a young person.

Statistics: Francis and Lankshear

4.8 There are also opportunities for young people to work for awards which enable their musical potential to be developed.

> The Royal School of Church Music offers awards for choristers which
> encompass 'an advanced level of musical attainment and encourage
> the highest standards of loyalty, industry and musicianship'.
> Candidates are recommended by their parish priest, or their choir-
> trainer and are examined by the RSCM. Successful candidates
> receive certificates and are entitled to wear the badges and ribbons
> which denote their achievement.

4.9   It is important to realise that as these young people are involved
on a weekly basis in their churches, the total number of hours and commitment this represents is enormous. Performing these offices and serving
the Church gives the young people an opportunity to come to know the
Church year, important rituals and scripture while worshipping and being
part of a spiritual community.

4.10   Special focus on youth work within a normal church worship programme has the effect of including young people.

> Every year for the last four years an ecumenical 'Youth Sunday' pack
> has been produced which gives ideas for a youth service and worship.
> In 1995 the National Youth Office distributed 2,226 packs to
> churches throughout England.

This work is a crucial part of many of these young people's religious journeys. However, some young people outside the Church who have no
knowledge of the tradition may find the Church liturgy and rituals strange.
In these cases considerable effort is needed to bridge this cultural gap
(see paragraphs 2.12-14). It is important for the Church to recognise this
work as worthy and understand that it can be a deep source of inspiration
to some young people who go from this into a lifelong Christian commitment.

Different congregations

4.11   In his book Building Missionary Congregations, Robert Warren writes
of different services and opportunities of outreach which spring up from
the main and more usual services that the Church conducts. Some
churches are holding services which are specifically for young people.
These youth congregations are said to be more attractive to the
unchurched young people than the traditional services. These provide a
real opportunity for outreach. There is a concern about splitting the
Church into different congregations and that this may result in some sort
of ageist differentiation. This is contrary to the basic assumption that the
Body of Christ is inclusive and heterogeneous. It is apparent that homo-
geneous groups such as a group of young people may bring a freshness

and vitality as well as contributing directly to growth (see paragraph 2.7). Churches which have multiple congregations are to be mindful of the need to provide an integrated holistic Christian witness whilst reaching out to specific groups and responding to their needs. Whilst it is important to hold these tensions, it is equally important that churches are looking for new ways to fulfil their mission within their own communities.

If there are lines of accountability it is important that the relationship between new initiatives and the Church is recognised. If the new group is part of the Church of England then there will be certain significant practices which show this connection.

> The following criteria, adapted from Breaking New Ground, pp. 32–3, may be helpful in exploring the connection between different congregations and the Church of England:
>
> 1. Is there commitment to the doctrine and practice of the Church of England as expressed in the Declaration of Assent?
>
> 2. Do the leaders of the group display an affirming attitude to the other traditions around them?
>
> 3. Do the leaders of the group use authorised forms of worship, being those allowed by the bishop's authority under section B of the Canons of the Church of England?
>
> 4. Do the leaders of the group have episcopal ordination, licence or authorisation to exercise their ministries in the local church and do those ministries include a life and teaching consonant with those normally experienced within the Church of England?
>
> 5. Does the group acknowledge episcopal leadership, and accept any financial or other diocesan obligations and generally participate in the common life of the diocese?
>
> These criteria provide helpful guidelines for determining whether a particular group is serious in its intention to serve the life of the Church of England.

4.12   These formal criteria are important in ensuring accountability, support and encouragement through establishing a connection with the Church. If these issues are addressed then there is the opportunity for considerable experimentation. Different locations can be used to reach those young people who are not familiar with the gospels and different approaches to worship can be used (see paragraph 2.37).

Alternative worship

4.13   Alternative worship services now happen in many of the major towns and cities in the United Kingdom. With names like BPM, The Late Service, Be Real, Wild Hope and Cooking Something Different, they have made steady headway, building up congregations and communities, frequently without any orchestrated publicity drive or launch strategy. They may not have any organised evangelistic tactics and sometimes they do not have support from local churches.

It is a phenomenon which almost invites misunderstanding. It is not a youth service or Experimental worship or Rave in the Nave or an evangelistic campaign. Those involved in this have been frustrated at the attempts to place this into one of the Church's pre-existing categories. At some point (it is suggested this may have been Greenbelt 1991) some people began to refer to 'Alternative Worship'.

> *On the first visit to a service, the main impression is visual. Screens and hanging fabrics, containing a multiplicity of colours, moving and static images continuously dominate the perceptions. There are other things: the type of music, often electronic, whose textures and range seem curiously attuned to the context of worship, smells, the postures adopted by worshippers, perhaps also their dress, style and hair. As the mental picture begins to fill up with detail, there is a growing appreciation that considerable technological complexity is sitting alongside simplicity and directness. The rituals — perhaps walking through patterns, tying a knot, or having one's hands or feet anointed — are introduced with simple, non-fussy directions. The emphasis is on allowing people to do what will help, liberate and encourage their worship rather than on the orchestration of a great event. The singing is normally simple, direct, chant-like. The structure of the event is not enormously complicated. Where something is rather obscure, its purpose is to invite reflection, perhaps teasing the worshippers to look deeper beyond the surface meaning. There is the occasional ritual joke. In many services, the steady, BPM-adjusted rhythm means that it would be possible on one level to participate merely by dancing. For many of those who stay, they have never before had an experience of Christian worship like it. It is as though they have come to a new place which they instantly recognise as home.*

> Paul Roberts, 'Papers from the Lambeth New Worship Day' (1995)

4.14   The movement amongst young people to express worship and church life within the frameworks of popular culture is both profound and strategic. 'The primary frontier which needs to be crossed in mission to young people is not so much a "generation gap" as a profound change in the overall culture' (Paul Roberts, ibid.).

In any innovative worship or new movements, there are no structures and systems of accountability and responsibility in place at the start. This means that there is a pressure on the integrity of the leaders who, because they are not in networks of accountability, are vulnerable and able to act unilaterally.

Alternative worship which is not necessarily networked into systems of accountability has received such criticism. For example, concern has been widespread in and outside the church about the alleged abuse within the congregation of the Nine O'Clock Service in Sheffield. However it has been widely recognised that the problem does not rest in the innovative worship but lies in the absence of accountability.

4.15   Leaders within the Church have sought both to affirm the presence of these services while at the same time to seek more accountable frameworks. Structures which offer accountability along with responsible guidance and ownership at diocesan level are needed and formal frameworks for the recognition of local liturgical experimentation need to be explored with Canon Law.

It is important that there are specialists who are able to resource the work and to explore the thinking in theology, liturgy and popular culture.

4.16   There is also a desire for some in the Church that ways are explored to bring alternative worship close to the whole work of the Church.

> Alternative worship springs from a healthy desire to take young people seriously, but equally it results from not taking the Church seriously enough.
>
> What we need is a holistic (in the biblical sense of the term) model of youth ministry, which recognises that one of our long term aims for young people is to see them integrated into one particular assembly of Christians, with all its variety in terms of age, gender, backgrounds, etc.
>
> Getting from where they are now to be fully and actively part of a local church is one of the great challenges of youth work today.
>
> Phil Moon, Vicar, Diocese of Norwich and member of the Working Party

Experimenting with worship

4.17   Creative use of the liturgy is important for all members of Church so that the worship is made anew for the congregation gathered (see paragraph 2.37). It is also important that this creativity includes the thoughts of young people. Where young people have been consulted there have been interesting changes to worship. The Taizé tradition has given inspiration to many services where a meditative style of worship, has been used (see paragraph 3.26). Rock culture has also been used to create worship, for example the 'Rave in the Nave' event in Ely Cathedral and other similar large scale events. Many of these events have a number of young people in the planning group, which helps ensure that what is offered is relevant and in tune with their needs.

> Rave in the Nave, Diocese of Ely
>
> 'Rave in the Nave' was conceived as an ecumenical event for the 14+ age group and was meant to be an event to which Christian young people would not be afraid to bring friends from outside the Church. The first took place in 1992. It runs on a Friday night in June from 8pm to 1am.
>
> Those involved in the planning have been from the Anglican, Methodist and Baptist Churches as well as the Boys' Brigade.
>
> The programme has included live bands on the main stage (created under the Octagon), a road show, a Nave programme which has included circus skills, human fly wall, Christian Aid fashion show, non-alcoholic bar, puppet theatre, fringe music and drama, etc. Last year the Nave was transformed into a street scene.
>
> As a contrast to this programme a separate, quieter, more reflective programme has been offered in the Lady Chapel. This has included Iona worship, Taizé worship, Gregorian Chant, Celtic harp, a string quartet, compline, etc.
>
> The climax of the event is at midnight when there is an hour of worship in an 'alternative' style. This has used large screen video, slides, live music, etc.
>
> Numbers at the event have risen to 1,100 with groups coming from all parts of East Anglia, Essex, the East Midlands and North London.

4.18   There are important messages given in when these services can take place. If they are tucked into a time when the 'real congregation' will not be affected there is an implicit message that the group is marginal and not part of the main church. Sometimes a congregation will start with a trial service and will work to integrate it into the main worship of the church. Using different locations can be effective in taking the gospel to places which are familiar and unthreatening to unchurched young people.

It is important that those planning this sort of worship have a good idea of who they are targeting and what they are trying to do through this work.

Consulting young people

4.19   As young people are not commonly part of parochial church councils or synod, their thoughts are often translated and anticipated by adults. This is not always effective and we suggest that it is easier, less confusing and more creative to ask the young people themselves.

> *Recently some members of the congregation got together to plan family services in the local church. Of the 12 members present all were over 40. When one of the members of the working party pointed this out efforts were made to recruit some younger people.*
>
> Member of the Working Party

4.20   A check of how many young people contribute to the worship of the Church often reveals how our worship is dominated by those over the age of forty. If young people are asked, they often bring a different perspective which can be appreciated by all, for example Taizé services.

Consultation has to be thought through first if it is to be effective. It is difficult for many young people to speak out in a large group of adults; it is much better if several young people contribute together and if an adult can work with them to prepare them for a meeting and chat through what has happened afterwards. What is desperately disappointing is for a young person to be plunged into a situation without the confidence or experience to cope. The situation can then be one of embarrassment and confusion rather than a creative addition to the worship of the Church.

Conclusion

4.21   Worship is central to the Church. If young people are going to be at the heart of the Church, they need to be part of planning and leading the worship. This sharing and dialogue can not only improve the lot of young people but can challenge and refresh the worship for the whole congregation. The dialogue with young people has to take into account their relative inexperience. If extra efforts are made to provide information and encourage and value their contributions, this will make the dialogue real. It is important for all members of the Church to make specific commitments to doing this (for example for a parish to include at least two young people on working parties to plan worship). These decisions need to be integral to the main objectives and aims of the Church which are discussed and agreed at parochial church councils and synod. For these decisions to be effective, adequate resources need to be located, including money, equipment and personnel.

It is important that worship is seen creatively and the response is flexible; at the same time it has to be part of a system of accountability and support. This support is through the structures of the Church and through an open and creative dialogue which embraces popular culture, experiments in liturgy and serious consultation with young people.

Young people in the structures of the Church

There is a tendency to believe on the part of adults that young people 'know it all'. This is untrue and young people say it's untrue. What young people say is that they have much to learn but also adults have much to learn from them . . . Young people do not want to destroy and rebuild, neither are they intent on being given everything. Rather their desire is to have an experience of the Church which is meaningful to them and to walk a pilgrim journey with either their peers and/or other adults.

Denis Tully (1995)

4.22   If young people are to be taken seriously in Church, then they need to have a say in how the Church operates and be part of its structure. If consultation and dialogue is a matter of choice rather than a right of young people, then this is reinforcing their marginal role within the Church.

The power gap

4.23   It is hard for most adults within their own congregations and churches to feel that they are 'powerful'. It often feels very difficult to do anything new, and with pressure on resources it can be difficult just to sustain the normal elements of church life (see paragraph 2.10).

Young people feel these pressures too. But they are compounded when they have no voice on Church decisions. They may not know *how, where,* and *when* Church matters are discussed and if they do get a chance to speak they may get flustered, confused and embarrassed.

Young people are faced with either fitting into the existing culture, or trying to change it with little knowledge of how they could make their views known and make the church experience more relevant to them. It is not surprising that the alternative of leaving is one to which many 12-to 20-year-olds resort.

4.24   In order to 'close' the power gap, young people (and others in the Church) need to know that their voice and comments are valued. They need to be informed explicitly of when, where and how they can contribute to the Church debate. They also need to be helped to frame items for the parochial church council meetings, encouraged to seek election and supported before, during and after any meeting or discussion they may have. The resolution for this to happen has been around for some time and the situation will only change when there are firm commitments to this end. For these commitments to be effective specific objectives have to be identified, resources have to be located to carry out these objectives, and the results of the action need to be monitored and assessed. For example, a diocesan synod could pass a resolution to allocate two places on synod for representatives under 25. They would then locate the resources to enable this to happen, perhaps the money to prepare a manifesto and maybe a past synod member could be nominated to give advice, support the candidate and act as sponsor. To assess how effective this proposed objective is, the diocese could nominate a person to submit a report to the next synod.

Young people at General Synod

For the last three years a group of young people have been to York to observe the work of the General Synod and to lead a session of worship. The National Youth Office has been working with this group to help them to make full use of this experience and to plan other ways of increasing young people's contribution to Church decision making. This has been with the close co-operation of the General Synod Office. Some of these young people are piloting some research in two dioceses to establish how many representatives in their parochial church councils or diocesan synod are under twenty-five.

During some research we have found twenty young adults on parochial church councils, two on deanery synod and one on diocesan synod. Not too bad – but not good enough.

The group are now working out ways in which these young representatives can be best supported in their work. They have organised a residential meeting and have identified a need for a parochial church council training day to equip young people to contribute successfully. They have also identified a role in being involved in clergy training days.

Youth synod held at Horsham with Bishop Lindsay Urwin

In September 1994 just over 50 teenagers from a variety of parishes in the episcopal area met for a 'Youth Synod' with Bishop Lindsay.

Planned with a small group of young adults, the group lived out Acts 2.42 with elements of teaching, fellowship, the breaking of bread and prayer.

In the context of this prayerful community life, participants met in groups on four occasions throughout the weekend to:

1. *Share their loves/hates about the local church.*

2. *Reflect about whether our faith affects day to day issues.*

3. *Share and reflect on our best experience of worship.*

4. *Discuss the problems of evangelism.*

Risks were taken! The groups did not have adult 'leaders' and it was a free for all. Not everything said was 'orthodox' — neither was it the last word, and in the final afternoon session Bishop Lindsay sought to draw the threads and thoughts of the weekend together. He used the opportunity to point out gently that Christians are not those who simply decide for themselves but stand under Scripture and the traditions of the Church.

Groups brought a statement and their ideas for the Church to the Bishop who silently sat in the Bishop's Chair. He promised the groups that their ideas would be sent to the clergy and parochial church councils of the episcopal area.

The bishop asked that two or three members of each parochial church council study the document, distil common themes, and present a summary with suggestions for action at a parochial church council meeting early in 1995. There have been positive responses from nearly all of the parishes.

Young people as representatives

4.25   The work described above can be seen as a step towards a full integration of young people into decision making in the Church. Another encouraging trend is that young people are increasingly part of parochial church councils and attend church meetings. This is very important in many ways, not only are young people given a voice, but they are also valued as full participating members of the Church, who have a worthwhile contribution to make.

Parish church councils representatives

There are 1,936 young people serving on parochial church councils.

14–17	102 men	108 women
18–21	523 men	307 women
22–25	1,161 men	928 women

Young people make up just under one per cent of PCC membership.

The total number of PCC members is 205,952 (94,233 male and 111,719 female).

Statistics: Francis and Lankshear

4.26   Young people will contribute best when they are informed, encouraged and listened to. To be most effective they also need support, which can come from the other members at meetings, who are sensitive to the new situation the young people are in. An existing committee member could be nominated to help explain procedures and ensure that the young person has proper access to information. A network of support of other young people who are fulfilling the same role in their own geographical area is also invaluable to share ideas and frustrations. Ideally several or all of these methods of support should be in place. It is important that as well as ensuring that young people have a voice, gender and different ethnic groups are also considered. This representation, like the young people's contribution to worship, has a double effect. Not only does it value and show that the Church thinks that young people are of worth, but the gifts of the young people and their energy are also released into the Church (see paragraph 2.28).

Young people as leaders

4.27   In Francis and Lankshear's research it was discovered that many young people are leaders in the Church. This seriously challenges the idea of young people as a passive group that need things doing for them.

Leadership by young people aged 14–25

Uniformed Organisations	3,427 men	4,935 women	total 8,362
Sunday School Leaders	1,719 men	6,766 women	total 8,485
CPAS Leaders	2,320 men	3,718 women	total 6,038
Youth Clubs	2,048 men	2,364 women	total 4,412
Parent/Toddler Groups	17 men	594 women	total 611
Play Group Leaders	6 men	368 women	total 374

Statistics: Francis and Lankshear

Interface with other organisations

4.28   There are many organisations which work with churches and are engaged in youth work. The Scout and Guide movements, the Girls' and Boys' Brigades and other uniformed organisations are committed to the spiritual as well as the physical and emotional development of their members. There can be opportunities where not only the leaders of these organisations are encouraged to contribute, but the members themselves could be consulted (see paragraphs 7.13 – 20).

There is much common territory between these groups and the Church which can be used creatively as part of the Church's mission.

Other organisations such as Anglican Youth, CPAS and Frontier Youth Trust are often working to similar agendas in the same parish and co-operative working can be very fruitful (see paragraph 7.24).

Partnerships are crucial to the Church's work with other Churches and institutions (see chapter 7).

Taking young people seriously

4.29   Young people must be taken seriously if they are to stay within the Church, or if the Church wants to attract young people into its work and mission. The Church must take seriously and engage in the issues that are important to young people. This dialogue which brings faith into ordinary life circumstances can be a crucial witness to young people, many of whom are quick to point out the hypocrisy of churches who fail to practise what they preach.

> The Church could be a place for people to come for help and either
> X receive that help or be referred to someone else. I feel that the Church
> has to recognise and acknowledge the problems that face young people
> today because they **are** the Church of today and they will be the
> Church of tomorrow.
>
> Susan Bruno, young person, Diocese of Chelmsford

4.30   Young people are living with unemployment, homelessness, family breakdown, bullying, issues around their sexuality, class, discrimination, pressure of exams, illiteracy, drugs and drink (see paragraph 1.4). It is painful to acknowledge these pressures and demands, but ignoring them means that we fail to take young people seriously. Engaging with them means that we create relationships, community and a chance to change. The implicit Christian mission behind much social action work can provide a powerful witness.

St Chad's Community Project, Diocese of Durham

St Chad's Community Project was set up in 1990 to work alongside the community in helping to identify strategies and resources for building up systems of self help and community development. It is situated in an area with 28 per cent unemployment with a large proportion of children (22 per cent between 0–15 years compared with a national average of 15 per cent); a growing Asian population, a large proportion of single parent families and an increasing solvent abuse and car crime problem. The area has one of the highest crime levels in the Northumbria Constabulary. The community project, housed within St Chad's Church, is deeply involved in work with the community on a number of levels.

Young people: The senior youth club members are encouraged to consider such issues as racism, drugs and sexuality in their weekly informal meetings (average attendance 15–20). We offer a supportive environment for teenagers who have few opportunities to socialise anywhere other than on the streets. Outdoor activities and weekend trips are offered occasionally. Young people are encouraged to train, volunteer their time and skills to the project or just to attend events and weekly sessions. The development of detached youth work helps to foster links with isolated young people in the locality.

Young people's potential – if you're good enough, you're old enough

4.31   Young people are a source of energy, enthusiasm and commitment and are essential not only to the future but to the present life of the Church and of our society. Failure to realise this and to integrate this potential into the life and work of the Church is not only a waste but also a great sadness (see paragraph 2.8).

Sometimes this potential may be difficult to locate and engage, for example when young people 'hang around' street corners. Detached youth work projects have shown time and time again that when these people are approached with openness and are given respect that they respond and readily share their enthusiasm, time and energy.

Water 4 Life, Diocese of Chelmsford

Emmanuel Youth Project runs from a church in East London. Thirteen members of the project although severely stressed by living in difficult circumstances (four were homeless, two were refugees from Somalia, and one has sickle cell anaemia) decided to try to help

*provide water for villages in Kenya. With the advice and guidance of
the project worker they raised over £36,000 for materials and air
fares for the Water 4 Life project and in the summer of 1995 flew to
Kenya to work with villages to build wells and tanks.*

*These self-styled 'non achievers up until this point' had gifts and a
potential that was recognised and used. Not only have the villagers in
Kenya benefitted from this project but it has been excellent in the personal growth of these young people. The example of these young people
as role models for others in the community is also exceptional.*

4.32   Young people do not expect the Church to wave a magic wand and
immediately lift any difficulties and solve all problems. What they are
asking is to be actively engaged in these problems and for their own gifts
and experience to be seen as part of the solution. Many young people have
ideas as to how to address the issues that they are dealing with (they do
it all of the time), but the Church can if it chooses play a part in this
process, both on the individual and community level (see paragraph 2.36).

Many motivated young people already give large amounts of time and
energy to community projects and to their churches. Some do this as part
of an organised scheme such as the Duke of Edinburgh awards, others
work in less structured ways. Many organisations work to match young
people who want to volunteer or donate their time and energies with
groups or churches working in the community. Some young people give
time to Careforce, which offers young people aged between 18 and 23
years placements with Christian projects.

Time for God

*Every year about 140 young people give up to a year of their time to
the Time for God scheme. They are placed in churches, projects and
other Christian organisations and receive their board and keep and a
little spending money. This voluntarily and freely-given time has
enhanced the places where they have been sent. The volunteers are
trained, supported and carefully matched so that their skills can
benefit the placement and they can learn and develop through the
work.*

4.33   Young people also contribute to worship, local fund raising and
community projects. They are often in the forefront of ecumenical partnerships and interfaith work.

There is also a tremendous amount that the Church and Christians
working in secular organisations can do for those outside the Church

without a faith. If the Church in its relation and partnerships with other organisations actively recognises the contribution that young people can make, then the Church will gain credibility. If, when the Church is in dialogue with other organisations, it sends young people as speakers, negotiators and advocates, then the vision of the Church will be one where young people are seen to be empowered. This message of empowerment and appreciation can be part of what the Church expects in its secular partnerships.

Conclusion

4.34   Robert Warren in *Building Missionary Congregations* predicts that the Church's best option for the future is in shifting from a Church life focus to a whole-life focus. 'It will mean concern not so much for the "work of ministry" as for the "ministry of work". It will be about equipping Church members to live out their humanity within the family and the work place (and lack of work) in response to God.'

There are many excellent initiatives working within the Church that honour young people and acknowledge their potential and their gifts. Developing new work involves proper commitment, taking the work seriously and giving enough resources and support to the work so that it succeeds. Some of this work is new and untried, and there needs to be a willingness to take risks. This work is best planned and managed in a partnership with young people that acknowledges their planning skills and their vision. Consultation and inclusion of young people in all Church processes is not only crucial to the the young people themselves but also to the life of the Church.

If the expectation of those in the Church is not just that young people have gifts but they have a space within the Church, in the worship and in the Church's decision-making, this gives a powerful message to those young people outside the Church and to our partner organisations.

5

Working with Relationships

Building relationships

Relationships in practice

It all started with the Junior Choir. Some of them wanted to know more about what they were doing in church and why they were doing it, so about six years ago a group of about half-a-dozen young people aged between 9 and 15 began meeting at my house after school on Tuesday afternoons.

And what do we do? Well, to put it simply we have Bible-based activities which teach them about their faith and what it means to be a Christian. Activities include plain Bible Study, drama, music, visits to the church, following a study course in Lent (we use the same course as the adult Lent groups), anything that can widen their knowledge.

The other thing that we do is to share a meal together. A proper meal that is: jacket potatoes, shepherd's pie, spaghetti bolognese, etc., that sort of thing, and always with cakes and buns for pudding! Communal eating really binds the group together and more than a few young people over the years have commented that the same effect should be felt by the church in the Eucharist.

Before they leave the group most of the young people are confirmed, and begin to play an active part in church life, something which gives me a great deal of pleasure and a sense of thankfulness for the opportunities I have had to share God's love with them.

Please pray for our young people. Our example, friendship and teaching is what they will carry into their adult lives and pass on to future generations.

Ruth Cooper, St Martin's Dorking, Diocese of Guildford

5.1   Relationships exist within the Church between all sorts of people. In the example above, Ruth realised that the young people wanted to know about the Church and she was prepared to work with the resources she had (herself and her house) to meet this need. This is not a complicated and difficult thing to do, it is simple outreach and sharing of Christian love.

Many people coming into church do so because of a relationship. In paragraph 2.31 we see that 'The call to a free, committed discipleship of Christ comes from friend to friend. We communicate through deeds and relationships before we communicate through words. Yet the very integrity of those relationships demands truth expressed in love'.

It is evident that if the mission of the Church includes young people then relationships have to be built across the age divide and the community of the Church has to include the community of young people.

> *We need to meet young people **where they are**, both physically and in terms of language, attitude, etc. We need to build relationships – that is we must listen to them – they must also listen to 'us'.*

> Bishop Stephen Venner, Bishop of Middleton

5.2   This two-way respect and willingness to enter into a real relationship is essential if the community of the Church is to be for people of all ages. Both young people and other Church members have to listen, and opportunities have to be made where both can have their say. These opportunities can be 'formal' within the Church's committees and in consultation with those in the Church who make decisions. The importance of these structures of communication is to allow real relationships of trust, understanding and respect to develop.

> *Respect for people is very important especially with young people . . . To respect people for **who** they are is vital. One of the main problems in life is people won't accept others for what they really are.*

> Young people on a youth work training course

5.3   Relationship forms the basis of all youth work and there are projects which focus exclusively on adults offering help and support to young people. Some of these projects are community-based and some have a specific interest as their focus.

> *Christians in Sport are working on ways that 'Coaches' linked to sports teams can begin to run Christian groups which they call 'huddle groups'. This is a friendship and relational outreach programme which has spread effectively through the USA and is now working in Great Britain.*

Peer relationships

5.4　　It is essential that adults take a responsibility for work with young people, and equally important that young people are responsible for the youth work. The balance between the two positions is arrived at by good communication with information being exchanged and by clear, negotiated action being agreed.

One of the main reasons that young people want to get together is because, like adults, they value what they can give and receive from each other. The Church has an opportunity of building on this basic desire of young people to create good, quality relationships across the age and culture gaps. Through these relationships the mission of the Church can be explored, shared and engaged with (see paragraph 2.31).

In the uniformed organisations the older members have clearly defined responsibilities and are expected to manage various tasks. Not only are they good role models whilst taking on these extra responsibilities, but it is also helpful in terms of their personal development.

A similar situation may arise in informal youth work settings as in a rural market town which has a club chiefly run by under 25-year-olds (see paragraph 5.27). Some dioceses have assistant leader schemes to develop the skills of young leaders.

> *Chelmsford Diocese Assistant Youth Worker Training*
>
> *The potential of young people who have been part of a youth club or project and want to work with young people is extended in this scheme. The diocesan youth officer organises weekends away where the basic youth work skills are offered together in a Christian framework. There are also 'Pick and Mix' weekends which are open to all youth workers. Here a range of skills, activities, discussions and workshops are offered to extend the workers and the youth work in the parishes.*

5.5　　Some of the most effective youth work is run by young people themselves.

> *An 'alternative service' is run under the eye of the chaplain at one of the large independent boarding schools. It is led by the 16- and 17 - year-olds with a visiting speaker. It attracts about 40–60 students and some parents each month. The music is vibrant, the teaching relevant. 'We see new people come each time' said the lead guitarist, aged 16.*

It is often only their own age group who have the ongoing relationships which enable them to invite their friends to 'come and see'. Young people want to be together, this is an end in itself. They draw strength from the group and value what they give and receive from each other. Often they attach more value to their friends than older people. Disloyalty or 'dobbing' can be enough to have them ousted from the group.

> For a terrible four days A was accused by her friends of having split on two boys on a geography field trip who had hidden in an underground car park and smoked a joint. She was sent to Coventry and wept her way through the days until it was proved and made public that she was not at fault.
>
> Working party member

For an insecure or sensitive young person such exclusion can be the worst kind of torture. They will often go to extreme lengths to avoid it.

5.6   Young people can be led astray by peer pressure just as much as they can be helped towards a living faith. The Church is in an unique position to offer a safe place in which to build good quality relationships and to offer the spiritual resources which change lives. Young people should be able to see in the Church good supportive peer relationships being modelled, 'the making of relationships of this kind is caught not taught' (Working party member).

Relationships and the future of the Church

5.7   Robert Warren in his book Building Missionary Congregations speaks of the loneliness of the individual in the West and the collapse of natural community. He writes 'Into the social vacuum the Church is sent in mission. It has the role of restoring natural community, albeit in a different form from previous patterns which have broken down, through the restoration of its own life'. He sees this focus on relationships and community as central to the Church's development. 'Particularly as the Church seeks to communicate with the under thirties, it must face the fact that they have little vision for or commitment to institutions as such' (see paragraph 2.19, section 6)

5.8   In the past the institution of the Church was attractive and the sense of belonging to a community with traditions and heritage was valued. Nowadays, institutions do not hold such sway with young people, an organisation is seen as valid not because of its history but by its work and direct engagement with the lives of young people (see paragraph 2.31). Relationships with others, both inside and outside the Church, is the measure of the Church's validity and integrity. These relationships can be informal, in that the Church or Church projects can be welcoming and attractive places where young people are noticed and wanted. The relationships can also be formal where young people's views are sought on how the Church or project is run and their opinions, knowledge and skills are taken seriously and valued. In this way the institution of the Church, and its work has a meaning and sense for the young today (see paragraph 2.10).

> *Young people respond to what most of us respond to — genuine, unsentimental concern and interest in them, being valued for what they are now rather than what they might become.*
>
> Anne Foreman, Evensong, Guildford 1994

5.9   This change of focus, which works through consultation and by acknowledging the gifts of all the individuals in the Church, can ensure that the structures and institution of the Church are there to help relationships develop rather than being ends in themselves. This would benefit all in the Church, not just young people.

5.10   Many people will have seen young people congregating naturally on street corners, in shopping precincts. Good youth work builds on this wish to be part of a group with shared aims. In many ways young people still have natural communities but the opportunity for expressing these in a longer and stronger commitment is weak. The Church has the opportunity to embrace these and use them within its work.

Companionship, support and sharing should be encouraged both at a peer level and between those of different ages for a more corporate Church and one which acknowledges the importance of relationships.

Peer relationships are also extremely important; if young people are thought of as a resource and allowed and encouraged to make relationships within the Church, this spirit and acceptance can provide a way in which other young people are brought to faith.

Anglican Youth

Anglican Youth (formerly the Anglican Young People's Association (AYPA)) is a national network within the Church of England — an organisation that is run by young people for young people. AY aims to help and encourage young people from all backgrounds to grow in faith, with opportunities to meet, share and explore together, locally nationally and internationally. AY is aimed at 15-25 year olds from all traditions within the Church of England, and offers support in setting up parish-based branches to help explore the four AY principles of fellowship, work, worship and education. National events and rallies provide opportunities for AY members to meet and work together.

Good youth work encourages people to work together and foster a sense of community. The potential for this way of working is not just to include and appreciate young people, but it can also provide a model of outreach to other groups in the community.

Relationships with parents

5.11   This report cannot be written without paying tribute to and emphasising the vitally important role played by Christian parents. They are there in their role of mentors, teachers and supporters of young people during the years when their faith is developing and becoming a first hand 'faith of their own'.

So often, in practice, it is Christian parents who support the youth worker, who encourage their son or daughter to attend events, who act as chauffeur to hordes of young people. They may end up late at night providing a 'sounding board' to other people's children as they prop up the kitchen table or sit on the stairs. The partnership between parents and the more formal 'youth worker' can be creative and supportive especially where the parents are sensitive to the needs of young people. It is important for many parents to know that the youth worker, who may be a mentor and confidant to their son or daughter, is working from a base of Christian values.

5.12   Some youth workers appreciate the role of parents and arrange 'parents' evenings' to discuss and come to understandings of the particular pressures that their children are experiencing. This can provide a forum where questions can be raised about the basic needs of teens and twenty-year-olds, for example their need for privacy and their own space. It can also offer an opportunity to vent some of the despair and frustration felt by many parents who are going through difficulties with their teenage sons and daughters.

The parents' role is vital in the life of a young person. The integrity of the parents' lives and faith has a crucial influence on young people.

Nurturing faith through relationships

5.13   Nurturing faith through relationships is a two-way growth in faith which happens as two people interact, care for each other and build each other up in the faith of Christ. It is important to understand that although at some times one party 'gives' and the other 'receives', these sustaining and positive actions are mutual and reciprocal. Both young and old can benefit from a sharing relationship like this where there is mutual respect and appreciation of what the other person has to offer.

If the term 'nurture' is to be used in work with young people it is important as acknowledged that this is a two-way process and young people are not seen as a passive, needy, resourceless group but are encouraged to bring their gifts to the relationship. The research in paragraph 4.24 and chapter 5 shows that the Church relies on young people for worship and leadership. They can also be very effective and sensitive carers and have a contribution in this respect to make to the life of the Church.

5.14   The most successful pieces of youth work will take place where there is a sense of respect between adults and young people and where the adults have helped to establish the work on the basis of equality. Nurture and a growth in faith from this sort of relationship is then two-way.

Outreach work – new initiatives to young people outside the Church

5.15   This work within the parish is dependent on good relations. Serving those within the community is essential but there is a call within the Church today for outreach.

'One aim of Christian youth work must be that young people become fully participating members of Christ's Church. Christianity is always personal but it also has to be corporate. Christian discipleship cannot be sustained in isolation by young or old.' (see paragraph 2.36)

Starting a project

All good youth work engages with the lives of young people, however there are times when Christians feel called to move beyond the boundaries of Church membership to 'reach out' to young people in the name of Christ.

Pete Ward, Working Party member and Archbishop's Adviser on Youth Ministry

5.16   There are many projects and pieces of work which attempt to move outside the Church and relate to young people 'where they are'. Some have an explicit message and see their prime objective as bringing the gospel to those outside the Church, others have an implicit Christian grounding and see their work in terms of sharing Christian love and concern. Where good practice is observed in both styles of work the Christian witness can be extremely important to the communities involved.

Targeted programmes

5.17   The recognition that 'outreach' to particular groups of young people will involve specific and targeted initiatives is a characteristic of emerging patterns of youth work within the Church. In most cases a new initiative arises because of the sense of distance between the Church and young people. In some cases this distance is identified by particular needs.

> *My Mum and Dad split up, and my mother's boyfriend moved in. There were problems with this, and he threatened me. Things got so bad that my mother told me to leave.*

> *I had a boyfriend and his mother offered me accommodation in the caravan in their garden, but I didn't feel comfortable there. My boyfriend's Mum told me about Sue Leach. When I met Sue, and she explained about her job I felt better that I wasn't on my own, and there was someone understanding to help me.*

> A user of the Rural Contact Project

> *This project is a free service provided for young people (16- to 25- year-olds) living in the rural areas of North and South Herefordshire, who may feel isolated and alone, in need of personal support, advice and information. The project is run in partnership between the Rural Development Commission, the Church of England Diocese of Hereford and the Youth Service. On average during a three month period the project works with 140 young people on a one-to-one basis.*

This project shows that young people living in small villages can feel isolated and have no access to help if they are in difficulties and seek guidance. The Church in partnership demonstrates an understanding of the difficulties of young people and is resourcing this outreach.

5.18   The following project is in an urban mixed area where young people are part of the work to support and resource the community.

> *St John's Youth Project in Southall, Middlesex, aims to maintain and develop a programme of activities open to all young people in Southall whatever their race, religion or cultural background. They have a special aim to work with girls and young women who may have little contact with anyone outside their family except for school or work. A full-time worker is employed and she runs and supports school clubs, Crusaders, worship groups, a girls club, a homework group, a senior club for 15- to 21-year-olds and visits and supports many individuals in the area. There is an Asian Christian Fellowship and a home group for young people over 15 years. They have organised a visit to the Czech Republic and have provided lighting and concreted part of the church car park for netball and 5-a-side football. The project started in 1987 and now over 200 young people are regularly involved.*

Connections with projects and the Church

5.19   One issue raised consistently by youth workers within the local community is the sense of ownership and connection between the work and the Church. This is crucial and where links are absent the work is unsupported and not so effective; where good links are made and maintained the work is potentially much more successful.

> One of the more longstanding community-based projects is the Shalom Youth Club in Grimsby, which has been run for the last 22 years by Anglican priest John Ellis. The project has been supported over a number of years by Lincoln Diocese and currently they supply one stipend to the centre worker who also acts as a deanery youth officer. In 1991 a 'Youth Church' was started which meets at 8.00 each Sunday evening in the Church centre. John Ellis summarises the aims of the project. 'Shalom is an agency for Christian informal education. It is primary task is educational. It is not a leisure provision – though it does make extensive use of leisure activities, nor is it a "soft policing" agency which views young people as a problem to be "kept off the streets" – though it is obvious that young people fully occupied and enjoying themselves are less likely to be involved in anti-social behaviour.
>
> The education undertaken is informal – that is to say it brings young people together on a voluntary basis and educates by means of a leisure setting. The education is also Christian in that the value system behind the policies and operation of the centre is Christian. Within the centre we aim to demonstrate what life is like when God is in charge – the kingdom of God.
>
> Shalom Annual Report, 1994

The work is clearly embedded in the local community and has obviously achieved a sense of trust and commitment to the people in that community. Through the informal education the project aims 'to meet the needs of young people in such a way that their efforts to become autonomous independent adults are strengthened and reinforced'.

> We understand the needs of young people to be fourfold:
>
> 1.   The need for love and security
>
> 2.   The need for responsibility
>
> 3.   The need for new experience
>
> 4.   The need for praise and recognition.

> It is our understanding that it is when these simple needs are denied that problems begin to occur and young people are thwarted in their journey to adulthood. As Christians we believe that these needs are best met within the context of a Christian world view.
>
> Shalom Project, with reference to Mia Kellmer Pringle

The Shalom Project also has an outreach worker who is involved in homelessness, a substance misuse group, a drug and support agency and works with careers workers. This work is in parallel with the Youth Church meeting and is integrated and supported by the local church.

5.20   There can be real difficulties where a project or a particular piece of outreach work is not networked with the local church. At the outset of any new piece of work consideration needs to be given as to how it relates to other churches and other organisations (religious and secular) within the area. Failure to do this means that work is not properly co-ordinated, can be set up without appropriate preparation and difficulties can arise which require a lot of effort to overcome.

Leadership

5.21   In building long-term successful work in the community it is clear that local people who can act as leaders are of prime importance. In some cases this can be a paid full-time worker; in others people living locally can work as voluntary helpers or leaders.

> In Ossett, West Yorkshire, a group of three middle aged women have for the last three years been going into the town centre on Tuesday evenings to meet the young people who congregate there. Through this long-term commitment and their attitude of genuine care and concern they have built up relationships with a group of young people. This year they plan to hold a series of small group meetings for some of the young people during Advent. At these meetings they hope to share their faith in a more personal way with the young people.
>
> On the Broxtowe estate in Nottingham, through the long-term evangelistic and pastoral work of the Church a team of five local people are voluntarily helping to run a youth group called The Zone. Through regular day to day contact with young people on the estate the outreach of the Church is reinforced.
>
> At St Chads Wood End in Coventry local youth and children's activities are run by professional people who are hired for a short term, e.g. one to three weeks at a time. The activities which might include a play

scheme, sports, or adventure activities are supported by a team of local people who help out voluntarily.

5.22   With all of these activities the wish to engage with young people has been addressed in different ways. The importance of long-term commitment and work cannot be over-emphasised. Leaders who live in an area bring a wealth of local knowledge and are already part of the community. These people deserve recognition and support in the valuable work they are doing. If this commitment and local knowledge can be fused with good safe practice, excellent work is achieved (see chapter 6).

Outreach

5.23   Within the Anglican Church, there has recently been a wave of new initiatives in outreach to the young people who have no involvement in Church. In many cases these projects are only two or at the most five years old and the churches supporting them are from the charismatic and evangelical traditions. They are significant indications that this energetic section of the Church is starting to engage seriously with the lives of young people. In some cases this involves running an event or night club where contact with young people can be made, for example 'Soul Survivor' in Watford and 'The Gap' in Swindon.

The style of such outreach and the resulting new Christians can make severe demands on local Anglican churches who are not prepared for an influx of large numbers with a distinct and different culture. Some projects have bridged this gap by a good flow of information from the project to the church and by working together on joint initiatives and projects. Where there are large differences in the culture and style of worship and ministry there needs to be understanding and constant endeavour and humility on both sides for good relations to work.

Integrating 'churched' and 'unchurched' young people

5.24   Several people wrote to the Working Party about the difficulty in bringing together 'non-church' and 'church' young people. A worker writes, 'It is not easy integrating non-church and church kids. There has been a fair bit of opposition from some church families about their youngsters mixing with the non-church group. There appears to be a fear that they are into drugs, sex etc . . . Evangelism is great for some until it impinges on their lives personally.'

Unfortunately there is no easy answer to this problem. There are projects where the congregation has been taken along with the outreach programme and so are prepared to accept radical changes in their worship and ministry to accommodate the new young people. There are other projects where the new young people are not so different to the existing culture of the church and have been able to integrate without great problems. A further alternative has been found by outreach projects who have worked with the local churches to develop separate churches or services specifically organised by and for young people.

Oxford Youth Works

In the middle of the 1980s a group of people in Oxford recognised that there was a need to try to develop a new way to reach out to young people who were currently not in any contact with the Church. The result was what Oxford Youth Works call 'The Relational Model of Youth Work'. This model is based on four very simple principles.

* *Christian adults meeting young people where the young people themselves hang out and feel comfortable.*

* *Christian adults forming supporting friendships based on the interests and activities of young people.*

* *Christian adults taking the time to share the message about Jesus in terms and ways that make sense within the cultural world of the young people.*

* *Young people who have heard the message of Jesus and responded to Him starting to form their own worship*

Ward, Adam and Levermore (1994)

Working relationships in small groups

Parish-based work

5.25   Thousands of churches are engaged in youth work without necessarily acknowledging it as such. Because many of these churches may only be working with a few young people they do not see this as 'youth work' or themselves as 'youth workers'. Some young people may be part of the choir, or are servers or bell ringers, some may be part of very small rural or inner city congregations, and much of this work is not noticed or acknowledged. Diocesan youth officers come into contact with some of these smaller initiatives and can support, offer training and resources when they are aware of the work.

A diocesan youth officer writes, 'A lot of youth work in the Worcester Diocese is done by one adult working at his/her home with a small group, three or four youngsters. They feel guilty because of their lack of size and unsupported because they feel no-one would be interested in helping them.'

In addition to Church-based work there is also a wide range of other work which takes place in the parishes including uniformed organisations and other Christian initiatives.

> There is more work with young people going on in the Church of England than might at first be supposed. It is not always systematic, it may often reach only a small group of young people and it may be limited in its approach, but to fail to confirm its existence and affirm what is going on would be to make light of the immense dedication both in time and commitment of those who work with young people in our parishes all over the country. To ignore it would also dishonour the quality of relationships which nurture our young people, our young people themselves and the life they give to our churches.

> Chris Dyer, Diocesan Youth Officer for Derby and member of the
> Working Party

National position

5.26   One way of ascertaining the extent of small group work can be by looking at one diocese and extending this picture into a national one. A survey in the Norwich Diocese revealed many rural churches in Norfolk have small groups of young people meeting together. Three hundred and twenty three young people are mailed directly and about eighty youth leaders request information for their small groups. These people are in addition to the thirty seven groups listed under group insurance and cater for over a thousand young people.

If as an estimate these eighty leaders work with five young people each there are about four hundred young people in the Diocese who work in an informal setting through their churches. If this pattern is repeated in the dioceses throughout England then the number of young people worked with in this way throughout England would be about sixteen thousand.

Resourcing parish work

5.27   It is extremely important that this work is acknowledged and valued as it is a crucial contact with young people who may be isolated. Many leaders are supported by their diocesan youth officers, but good training, support, shared activities and joint efforts to maintain standards in the work has to be realistically resourced. A diocese of six hundred parishes which may have only one diocesan youth officer must expect work to be prioritised to produce the best outcomes. Thus the specialist skills of the diocesan youth officer may not be available to many of the parishes in the diocese.

It was interesting to find myself at a small market town last Friday with the vicar, now over 60 and a couple of 25-year-olds running a group of over 20 young people aged 11-14. He talked of the difficulties of keeping the group going and finding leaders, yet every week they get over 20 for a varied programme. Whilst the numbers are probably higher here than in villages it is a similar scenario. His real concern is for the 14+ of which they have a few in the church and for the 16+ who sit at the west door of the church drinking and sniffing glue. He could see the needs but felt powerless, and generally was resourceless to respond.

David Green, Diocesan Youth Officer, Norwich Diocese

There are ways of working with young people in these sorts of situations. Opportunities can be discussed and ideas given at training events. With good support some of these ideas can be put into practice, and leaders and clergy can be encouraged to reach out to the young people hanging around outside the church. Some dioceses have teams of people who can give an input to worship and youth work. Larger events are often run by the diocese, enabling young people to try new experiences and work in larger groups. These diocesan initiatives need financial support and acknowledgement.

5.28   Many national Christian organisations work with small groups at parish level and have remits to share the gospel with young people outside the Church. Resources between Christian organisations, secular work initiatives and local education authorities can be shared, providing excellent opportunities to use specialist projects and services to help inform young people and youth workers, for example drug/alcohol dependency services. Many Christians who work in secular posts and are in contact with young people are an untapped resource for the Church. Much of this work goes on unnoticed as the Church does not have any formal way of acknowledging and supporting this calling.

5.29   A large amount of work happens in small groups in parishes, where initiatives through fairly low-key relationships have been described as 'the backbone of the Church's work with young people'. However, as they are not announced or formally acknowledged as being 'youth work', by the leaders, the young people, the incumbent, the deanery, the diocese, or nationally, the work cannot be resourced or supported. This type of work may be the only contact young people have with the Church, particularly in rural settings, and it is important that ways of valuing, supporting and resourcing it are found. Without this recognition the work cannot be extended.

Baptism, confirmation and marriage

5.30   For many people, their only contact and link with the Church is to attend baptisms, weddings and funerals. These contacts are crucial in sharing the message of the Church and are an opportunity for the church to enter into a relationship with young people. Preparation classes offer not only the chance to teach something of the gospel to a young person, but can also show Christian love and care, which is the basis of the Church community.

Marriage

5.31   The Church has always had a role in society to 'Hatch, Match and Dispatch', which may be the only times young people are drawn into the worshipping community of the Church. The research of Francis and Lankshear has shown the very large number of contacts with young people who come to get married in the Church.

Young people who are brides and grooms in 1994

Brides	16-21 years	7,124	22-25 years	32,290	total	39,414
Grooms	16-21 years	2,773	22-25 years	27,344	total	30,117

Total of Brides and Grooms under 25 69,531

Statistics: Francis and Lankshear

5.32   A church with a good marriage preparation programme is in effect doing good youth work, especially with the older group of young people. For those within the church the sacrament of marriage can be incorporated as part of a spiritual and social development. For those who do not regularly attend Church, this can be an important point of contact, an opportunity for these young people to see the love and mission of the Church.

Baptism

5.33   *Young people attending baptism classes, being baptised and confirmed*

	Baptism Classes	Baptised	Confirmed
10–13 years	277	2,275	17,639
14–17 years	266	1,126	8,613
18–21 years	2,003	719	906
22–25 years	19,371	1,120	1,307
Total	21,917	5,240	28,465

The total number of people baptised is 956,125 so the young people between the ages of 10 and 25 represent .5 per cent of this total.

The total number confirmed is 47,149 with the young people being 60 per cent of this total.

(*Statistics: Francis and Lankshear, 1994*)

The table above reveals some interesting patterns. Many of the people in the 22–25 year band who attend baptism classes are there not on their own behalf but are young parents attending with their children. As with marriage, contact with young people at this time is really significant; good work done at baptism classes can confirm the mission of the Church and be an opportunity of working alongside young people who may not be members of the congregation. Working with young parents also builds a link which can evolve into welcoming and working with their children. This link is especially important for those who do not fall into the traditional picture of the family; young single mothers or fathers, or couples who are not married can be welcomed into the Church through the baptism of their children.

Confirmation

5.34   Confirmation preparation is seen by many churches as an opportunity to work with young people to explore and affirm their faith before welcoming them into full membership of the Church through the Eucharist. Confirmation marks the integration of the experience of conversion together with personal development and heralds the beginning of a person's discipleship (see paragraph 2.34) The pattern of birth, baptism, confirmation and communion is followed by most churches, although some do welcome children to the Eucharist as part of exploring different liturgies. The age at which a person is confirmed can vary, reflecting different churchmanship. From the table above it is interesting and possibly worrying to note that so few young people are confirmed between the ages of 14 and 21 years. The sense of not really belonging and not being a part of the main Church may be one of the reasons for this unwillingness to be confirmed. Another reason may be as a result of the Church worship pattern, which is discussed below.

Confirmation trends

5.35   There has been a steady fall in the number of people being confirmed in the Church of England. Lankshear (1993) demonstrates that while 1,659,548 individuals were confirmed in the decade between 1958 and 1967 the figure fell to 1,053,963 between 1968 and 1977 and to 844,087 between 1978 and 1987.

At the same time Francis and Lankshear argue from research in one diocese (Chelmsford) that the percentage of teenagers being confirmed has steadily decreased. In the three-year period between 1981 and 1983 young people accounted for 57.6 per cent of candidates, between 1984 and 1986 52.4 per cent and between 1987 and 1989, 46.9 per cent.

Another significant trend is that the number of candidates under 13 is increasing proportionally to those between 13 and 21. Between 1981 and 1983 those between 13 and 21 outnumbered the under 13s whilst during the period between 1987 and 1989 the two age groups were represented by equal numbers of candidates (Francis and Lankshear, 1993).

These figures show that the number of young people between 13 and 21 who are coming forward to be confirmed is decreasing rapidly, during 1987 and 1989 only 22.4 per cent of the total candidates presenting for confirmation were between 13 and 21. If confirmation is seen as the initiation or the rite of passage into the Church, this does not bode well for the future membership of the Church.

5.36   One way that confirmation can bring people into a relationship with the church is noted in a recent report, *On the Way*, which explores confirmation and initiation within the Church. It acknowledges that most people join a worshipping community through a personal contact, and relationship and companionship is built into the catechumenate scheme.

> *An essential part of the faith journey as envisaged in the catechumenate is that it should be an accompanied one. The role of 'sponsor' is therefore highly significant, essentially it is an Emmaus Road experience. The candidate and sponsor walk together. The sponsor – a lay person – cares for and prays for the candidate and introduces the candidate to the rites (the process of confirmation). The sponsor shares his/her own faith journey and helps to articulate and thus evaluate and value his/her own. (p. 46)*

Essentially this role of companionship, support and sharing should be encouraged between those of different ages for a more corporate Church and should be seen as applying to young people and not just adults.

Confirmation practice
5.37   Francis and Lankshear demonstrated two distinct confirmation practices in their research: those churches which confirmed younger candidates and those who tended to confirm adult candidates. The churches that were more focused on the Eucharist as being central to their worship tended to confirm younger candidates. Churches that were experiencing growth had more adult candidates.

Both patterns pose questions for the work with 13- to 21-year-olds. Statistically the churches that confirm younger people do not necessarily retain 13- to 21-year-olds in their regular congregations. Some people have said that many see confirmation as a 'rite of passage' out of the Church rather than as a ceremony of welcome into the worshipping community. There is an issue about helping the young people to continue as part of the main Church and to see their confirmation as part of a process of continual learning and relationship which will continue throughout their adult lives (see paragraphs 2.13-14 and 2.21-23). This has been addressed in a number of different ways.

Challenger Scheme, Diocese of Truro

'Challengers' is a structured ecumenical programme of tasks and challenges designed to enable and encourage spiritual growth, and to encourage a sense of belonging to the Church and the community. The scheme starts with simple challenges (e.g. to learn a Psalm) that can be attempted by 6-year-olds who regularly attend church, and continues through a series of challenges to the gold challenge (e.g. to go on a two day retreat) which is expected to be post-confirmation and can be attempted by those over 16 years old. Each challenge has several small projects to attempt and those on the challenge have a tutor who helps and assists them through. The relationship of challenger and tutor is seen as an important link and encouragement to the church and the scheme helps to inform and enable young people to become a part of the Church and the wider community.

The one and only young person in a church congregation in a small church up on Bodmin Moor is as important to the church as the 50 or so members of an active sunday school and youth group in one of our town churches. To help them realise just how important they are and to encourage them in their spiritual growth we have devised a graded programme of challenges around the theme of 'Belonging'.

5.38   Those churches that do confirm more adults may see the commitment at a later age as one that is more mature and reflective. Here there is an issue of whether this delayed confirmation, if it is also accompanied by no communion, is denying the young people access to the full life of the Church.

In all cases the time of reflection, teaching and contact with people within the church is valuable. Although pre-confirmation work has traditionally been seen as work for the incumbent and based on teaching and informing, some schemes are much more interactive, for example *Discovery Wheel* (published in 1994), an exploratory method emphasises that those leading confirmation classes are encouraged to find different ways to work with the young people.

Linking young people with an adult who sponsors them is also valuable in building relationships and helping recently confirmed people to be part of the church. These friendships can also work to form a solid church community.

There has been much work recently on restoring the adult catechumenate, and it should be possible to integrate some of these ideas with Church youth work (see paragraph 2.16).

Post-confirmation work

5.39   Many dioceses run post-confirmation weekends where young people can reflect and discuss their work and role in the Church. Some combine this with a visit from the bishop who confirmed the young people. This continuity and commitment to young people as they join the Church is a valuable part of a structural caring relationship.

> *Diocese of Derby*
>
> *Following concern from parishes about what happened to young people after confirmation, the diocesan youth officer and the warden of the diocesan youth house co-operated to set up an annual weekend for anyone up to the age of 18 who had been confirmed in the last year.*
>
> *The weekend is run at Champion House, Edale, by the suffragan bishop, DYO, warden of Champion House, volunteer youth leaders and older young people (i.e. around 17).*
>
> *Invitations are sent individually by the confirming bishop (via the incumbent) to young people they have confirmed. The weekend, called The Next Step, encourages the young people to consider what confirmation meant to them and what the next step is in their spiritual lives. The personal interest of the bishops involved has been much appreciated and some young people who have attended this have come back to further weekends at the house.*

Conclusion

5.40   Relationships are central to the life of the Church. The quality of relationships that young people have in the Church is a crucial element in how they engage with the Church.

> *Christ's ministry and healing compassion was open to all, whatever, their response to him; but not ignoring their response. Similarly the Church's youth work will always be committed to the personal devel-*

opment of young people irrespective of their view of Christ; but it can never depart from its understanding that true humanity finds its fulfilment in relationship with him.

paragraph 2.23

5.41   A relationship starts by acknowledging and affirming people where they are, and then sharing, with mutual respect, things that are important. Many young people have a tremendous responsibility and concern for the world and are eager to explore their spirituality and faith. If the Church and older Christians are aware of this and are open to what young people bring to the relationship, there are possibilities of change and growth. Also, the Church will be more relevant to young people and they will want to be part of it. This is happening in some churches and Anglican projects and is worth sharing throughout the Church.

5.42   In this chapter the relationships between young people and the importance of young people as leaders and role models for each other has been explored. Parents are shown as vital to the life and faith of a young person and the nurturing of faith by parents, youth workers and others is an essential part of the responsibility of the Church.

5.43   The Church of England has a responsibility to people in England that is being addressed by the many individuals and projects engaged in forming relationships with those who do not ordinarily come to church. The aspect of relationship is also central to the thousands of small pieces of youth work that go largely unnoticed in churches all over England. There is an enormous opportunity to extend and expand this work by affirming it and offering recognition, proper resources, support and training to those engaged in it.

5.44   Lastly, the opportunities of the Church as people celebrate the sacraments of baptism, confirmation and marriage have been explored: opportunities not only of sharing the word of God but also the care, concern and love of God. Many parishes use the preparation time for these events to build up relationships of mutual trust and respect and offer a real welcome and sense of belonging to those wanting to use the services. There are schemes locally or at a diocesan level which offer invitations following baptism, marriage or confirmation to young people to reaffirm the relationship between them and the Church.

All of these initiatives need resources. It is possible to share training and resources with other religious or secular organisations. However, if the Church wants to build relationships, it is vital that the work at all levels is adequately supported and funded. In the words of a young person, 'The Church must put its money where its mouth is.'

6

Working with Those who Work with Young People

Recognising and affirming the ministry of youth workers

> Over the past eight years I have often been asked why I don't have a
> 'real' or a 'proper' job. Why do I just work with young people? Indeed,
> I have asked that question myself many times at 2 o'clock in the
> morning whilst away with a difficult group of youngsters who won't
> sleep. There are of course many answers. The main one, though, is the
> young people themselves. Someone took time to work with me as a
> rebellious fifteen year old who had never been to church in his life and
> showed me that God cares through his Church. Someone valued me
> as a young person, took me seriously. Someone took time to provide
> a youth facility in the local church for fifty local lads with nothing to
> do, and put up with the damage we caused and the abuse we gave.
> Someone showed me the Church in action serving the community in
> which it lives.

> Duncan Green, Diocesan Youth Officer for Chelmsford: extracts
> from a sermon preached at Westminster Abbey Evensong,
> 26 February 1995, taken from *Anglican World*, 1995

6.1   Francis and Lankshear's research shows that there are thousands
of people working with young people in congregations throughout
England. This averages out to at least one person in every parish who is
willing to show 'the Church in action' by committing themselves to young
people. This work can be very difficult, not least because it is largely
unrecognised. Turning out to a small rural youth club on a winter's night
with few resources and minimal parish support is difficult enough for the
young people, let alone the leaders. Talking to young people outside the
church in an inner city area can be daunting and dangerous. Working with
young people who are experiencing family breakups, pressure of exams,
homelessness, unemployment, racism, sexism or abuse is very tough.

I came off the phone feeling angry and frustrated. Here was a colleague, a voluntary parish youth worker, who had given five years slog and commitment to setting up a parish youth club, and who, at the end of the day, felt that the clergy and parishioners simply didn't care, let alone show any understanding of the cultural and spiritual problems he had struggled with. He left the club feeling unvalued and wondering what sort of an institution the Church was to be so insensitive and thankless. I hoped that he would not find his Christian faith so badly bruised that he gave it up, but I couldn't blame him if he did.

Graham Richards, Diocesan Youth Officer, York Diocese, from *York Talk*, Spring 1995

6.2   If the Church is to be a Church in action in the community it must recognise the gifts and commitments of youth workers and affirm and support them. Many people writing into the report spoke of how youth leaders and workers deserve to be valued. A vicar from Northamptonshire writes, 'Anyone who works with young people needs to be trained, evaluated, supported, nurtured and loved every bit as much as their clients'.

The nature of work with young people
6.3   There is huge range of youth work going on in the Church of England. Many churches are involved in work with uniformed organisations, with clubs or run Sunday Schools. Every church has some contact with young people if only when they are married or bring their children to be baptised (see paragraph 5.30-38). Furthermore, many Christians are called to work with young people in the secular world and this needs acknowledging, supporting and affirming. All of these contacts can be used to build up relationships with young people.

Churches that do more work with young people will have specified youth workers whose work covers many different areas.

It is clear from submissions received by the Working Party that youth workers, whether voluntary or paid, part-time or full-time, undertake a range of different roles and tasks including those of:-

advocate	*enabler*	*friend*	*adviser*	*counsellor*
organiser	*teacher*	*evangelist*	*group worker*	*manager*
trainer	*communicator*	*observer*	*report-writer*	*researcher*

Sub-group of the Working Party

There are core skills, values and knowledge that undergird work with young people. These can be acquired through experience, learned in training and applied to particular settings. Underlying all these skills is a central value in youth work of respect for young people. Christian youth work starts with this respect and draws from the message of the gospel and the power of God's love. The experience of workers in youth work in the inner city, and in rural settings or dealing with special circumstances such as homelessness, racism and unemployment can be shared and used to help young people (see chapter 1).

6.4 The role of the youth worker, and the nature of youth work undertaken, can be shaped and enhanced by the degree of contact and involvement with the diocesan youth officer/adviser, with a range of other Christian and non-Christian agencies, with other voluntary youth organisations, and with the LEA Youth/Community Services.

Working in partnership with other agencies can work towards the following outcomes:

- *Joint funding and delivery of projects/training/events*
- *Co-ordination of provision to maximise use of resources*
- *Opportunities for young people and the youth workers to come together*
- *Focus on non-Church young people and their social/welfare needs*
- *Focus on the nurture of young people within the Church*
- *Focus on evangelism and evangelistic events*

Sub-group of the Working Party

Such contacts can offer affiliation to local, regional and national networks and structures. These can be supportive, provide access to training and be affirming to an individual youth worker's ministry. Working relationships with other organisations help to make the Church better understood and part of mainstream youth work as well as giving specific opportunities to individuals and groups.

Opportunities include:

- *Spectrum training programmes for part-time youth workers*
- *Access to national training events*

- Recognition as part of the wider contribution being made to the lives of young people

- Awareness of opportunities available locally and nationally for young people

Sub-group of the Working Party

6.5 It is important that the work that the Church undertakes is safe for young people, and follows good practice. *Safe from Harm* and the 1989 Children Act have implications for youth work in the Church (see paragraphs 6.42-46, and 2.36, section 2) and many dioceses have integrated this into the support and training of youth workers.

Who does this work?

6.6 Youth work happens in a variety of ways and involves different people. In churches that take this work seriously a response might be 'all are involved in youth work' and that everyone takes responsibility in maintaining a welcome, support, resources and prayer for the work to happen.

People are usually designated for this work, and the commitment can range from a member of the congregation befriending a young person, to a team of full-time youth workers engaged on a specific project. Although the scale of the work may be different, all youth workers need recognition, support, accountability, resources, and for the Church or organisation to understand their aims and objectives.

The youth work of the Church is a crucial part of its ministry and mission, and those who work with young people should have the very best skills, abilities and commitment. It is also important that these people do not just drift into the work but that the Church takes this aspect of its mission seriously. If this is the case then workers can be matched carefully with the tasks that are required of them; for some this will be a full-time youth work post; for others it will be a simple or regular task which is also important to the overall youth work of the church.

Often the context and the content of the youth workers' work will be set by policy decisions of their PCC. In some instances the worker may fail to gain a clear understanding of what the church aims to do in its youth work. This lack of clarity regarding the role and function of the youth worker can create unrealistic and confused expectations of both the work and the worker.

If the Church is to honour the thousands of people who offer their gifts, skills, and talents in serving young people then a strong plea has emerged for:

- Each parish to be clear about its aim and mission in seeking to work with, and for young people (whether those young people are 'within' the church or 'external' to it).

- Care to be taken in the recruitment and appointment of both voluntary and paid youth workers in accordance with diocesan/ national guidelines.

- All youth workers, paid and voluntary, to be adequately supported and trained.

- The Church to recognise youth work as a specialist ministry, affording it appropriate status and resourcing.

Sub-group of the Working Party

Volunteers in youth work

6.7   A tremendous amount of youth work is done by volunteers in the Church. Their recruitment and retention has become a cause for concern in many organisations – and the Church and youth work agencies are no exception to this.

Over the last five years those people fortunate enough to be in work have had more expected of them at work – more time, stress, responsibility etc. . . It could be argued that this has had an effect on recruiting people to help/volunteer for youth work.

Member of the Working Party

6.8   In recent years there has been a change in the nature of volunteering and people responding to the report have stressed that this work is voluntary but not amateur. The appointment, support and training of volunteers is given far greater attention than previously. The volunteer's role needs to be clearly defined, as do lines of responsibility. A process of reviewing, evaluating and appraisal needs to discussed and agreed from the outset.

In the context of youth work, evidence suggests that voluntary workers value situations where their:

- *job is well defined*

- *lines of responsibility and accountability are clear*

- *appointment is for a fixed period and a process of appraisal exists*

- *training is seen as an essential part of their development*

- *youth work is valued and formally recognised.*

Sub-group of the Working Party

The following example shows where the aims of the work have been clearly negotiated. The responsibilities of the workers and what is expected of them are also apparent in the description of the club.

The Parish of St Peter's, Bengeworth, Diocese of Worcester

Bengeworth Youth Club consists of 33 young people and eight leaders. Our aim is to provide a safe and supportive environment for all young people in Bengeworth from the ages of 10 to 18 regardless of religious allegiance. The club meets every Thursday evening in a church building. There are a variety of games and a meeting area to talk and have refreshments. As well as the weekly meetings we aim to take the young people out for weekends, days and evenings. Whilst we are open to all we maintain our Christian ethos in a 'worship slot' which is entirely organised by the young people.

The club is run on an enabling pattern with the young people forming a committee to run the club and devise policy. They also run a tuck shop, ordering, pricing stock and keeping accounts. This enabling and collaborative structure allows valuable skills to be acquired in a nurturing environment. We are committed to the personal development of the leaders, most of whom have been on the Spectrum youth leaders' course. The leaders meet monthly to discuss feelings, problems and ideas.

Networking has been important for the club on a county and local basis – liaising with the voluntary and statutory sectors. This networking has borne fruits in the acquisition of funds and equipment.

What does the volunteer do?

6.9   The volunteer's role is dependent on the nature of the work, but key issues for success include support, accountability, responsibility, training and evaluation. With these in place it is much easier for the volunteers to work to a high standard and find the work worthwhile, and a spirit of achievement and commitment will exist in the work.

Training

6.10   Responses to the Working Party frequently stressed the value and importance of training for voluntary youth workers. Churches with large teams of volunteers are often able to arrange training independently by using skilled trainers from their diocese or other agencies. However, volunteers are more likely to depend upon training offered through diocesan specialist/sector ministry departments, which bring together youth workers from neighbouring parishes, across their deanery or even a whole diocese.

Important aspects of training valued by volunteers:

- *learning new skills which help directly with their youth group programme*

- *having access to new resources*

- *learning from what other volunteers do in their work*

- *discovering new ideas for all aspects of their youth work programme including worship, Bible study and prayer*

- *discovering their strengths and gaining confidence to tackle new training opportunities*

- *discovering that they are part of a much greater number of people serving God and the Church in youth work*

Sub-group of the Working Party

6.11   Many volunteers have completed the Spectrum course, an ecumenical training programme for part-time youth workers which was written by an ecumenical group of denominational youth officers and has been delivered successfully throughout the country by teams of trainers from each of the major denominations. The diocesan youth officer network has played a significant and crucial role in managing these courses. The Spectrum course can also been used as a good introductory programme for prospective youth workers who may be in a full-time placement attached to a church.

Spectrum training course outline:

- *Being a youth worker (1)*

- *Development in adolescence*

- *Group work day*

- *Leadership*

- *Communication*

- *Being a youth worker (2)*

- *Pastoral care*

- *Spirituality*

- Support of youth workers
- The Church, community and young people
- Working relationships
- Management

Support

6.12   A volunteer engaged in youth work must receive proper support, both practical and spiritual (see paragraph 2.36, section 1). The more intense or difficult the work, the greater should be the support. There are two types of practical support, formal or informal; a youth work project should have both. Formal support involves other people being responsible for aspects of the work. It is the structure in which the volunteer works. Youth clubs or ventures can be well served by management committees which provide a reference point for the work, help with resources, and support and line manage all elements of the work. If the work is not so extensive the formal support may be simply a person whom the youth worker sees regularly. It is especially important for the volunteer to know who s/he is directly responsible to in the event of an accident or emergency. For work in the parish the incumbent and PCC provide formal support.

Youth work in a parish often succeeds or fails on the support or lack of it offered by the PCC and the incumbent. The Shalom Project in Grimsby (see paragraph 5.19) which has been running for over 22 years, is an example of how an initiative which is well integrated into the church and the parish can develop and last.

6.13   Informal support often happens in the general attitude of the church and other people to the work, and by being supported by friends and colleagues. One aspect of formal support should ensure that informal support is in place.

It is important that confidential issues relating to young people are treated with respect and sensitive information be initially shared only with the person the worker is immediately responsible to. Further sharing of the information should be on a 'need to know' basis and, unless there are good reasons for not doing so, should be in full consultation with the young person or people.

Spiritual support can be part of the practical support agencies described above and/or it can be provided in other ways. Some workers have spiritual directors, prayer groups that regularly meet to focus on issues within the project, or have a whole prayer ministry within the church directed at the work with young people. Some dioceses have a prayer focus on their work with young people. At all levels of the Church, from the individual to the national, there is a need to support youth work through prayer.

Most dioceses have a diocesan youth officer who can offer support to the youth worker and the youth work in the diocese and can locate professional and spiritual help.

Deanery Youth Initiative, Diocese of Wakefield

When I came to the Diocese it soon became apparent that the youth work scene was typical of that in many other dioceses. In each deanery there might be one or two churches with a youth group of some kind and the rest struggling to keep hold of the few young people, if any, that were involved in the life of the church. In order to provide young people with a place in the church it was important to address the situation of the 'oasis in the desert'. I decided to use the strength of the deanery system to do this. If St Pews had thriving youth work, whilst St Pulpits had nothing, perhaps by working together they could learn, work and grow.

The Initiative aims to build on existing youth work in any given deanery, using skills and experience of up and running youth groups to base deanery youth work on.

The Initiative exists to:

1. *Put on at least two deanery events a year.*

2. *Address training needs of leaders within their own cultural context. What is needed in Huddersfield might not hit the spot in Pontefract.*

3. *Provide a forum for networking and mutual support for youth workers.*

4. *Provide an interface between the diocesan youth officer, the deanery and individual parishes.*

5. *Eventually to establish networks of youth forums, called WAM groups (What About Me!), throughout the diocese.*

The project has been running in Huddersfield deanery and has had the following spin offs:

1. *The profile of youth work has been raised in the deanery.*

2. *Sharing of talents, premises, skills and experience has taken place.*

3. *Other deaneries have had their appetites whetted.*

4. *We have had fun (almost).*

5. *We are left feeling 'what can we do next?'.*

Young people as volunteers

6.14   Young people volunteer their time and their energies for Christian work. Paragraph 4.27 shows that over 28,000 leadership roles are held by young people in the 16,000 worshipping congregations in the Church of England (see paragraphs 4.31–3 and 7.13). Further work is done by young people, including visiting, gardening, helping with fund raising and leading Bible study groups.

> In one parish in Horsham a 15-year-old boy is host for an all age Lent house group. The Bishop of Horsham says the youth work we are doing is not **for** young people but **with** young people and sees the work in his episcopal area fostering a youthfulness of spirit among all people.

Employing a paid youth worker

6.15   Submissions to the Working Party have highlighted the steady growth in the number of paid full-time and part-time youth workers, who are employed or supported by individual parishes, groups of parishes or deaneries. There is also a growing number of Anglicans employed in full-time youth work or youth ministry with other agencies both Christian and secular.

> St John's Woodbridge, Diocese of St Edmundsbury and Ipswich
>
> Employing a full-time youth worker
>
> We have heard 'horror stories' from youth workers about youth workers: salaries that are irregularly paid pittances, slum accommodation, no job description, expected to fulfil the joint roles of verger and curate, impossibly long hours, no guidance and support. We determined this would not happen at St John's. It has meant, among other things, brushing up on our employment law and drafting plenty of paperwork, from disciplinary and grievance procedure, health and safety policy, tenancy agreement, salary scale, monthly budget summaries etc. etc.
>
> The following points have been useful to us in appointing our own worker:
>
> - Be clear about what you want to achieve through a youth worker . . .
> - . . . and in what time scale
> - Plan, plan and plan again
> - Project ownership is central

- *As far as possible fund your own work, but tell others what you are doing*
- *Set your budget before fundraising*
- *Spend time and energy on recruitment*
- *Support – this works both ways*
- *Employment and management issues cannot be ignored*

St John's voted to employ a full-time youth worker at the PCC early in 1993. A youth worker was employed from May 1994

6.16   The introduction of the 1989 Children Act and the Home Office Report *Safe from Harm* have had, and will continue to have, an impact upon youth work practice. Many dioceses have produced guidelines for good youth work practice which refer to the need for care in appointing both voluntary and paid youth workers.

Suggestions regarding Recruitment/Support/Training

There is a need for:

- *'approval' of those working with young people*
- *clear job descriptions for youth workers*
- *clear statement of 'safe' practices in all aspects of youth work undertaken*
- *youth work programme to be approved by management body (PCC)*
- *appropriate insurance to be in force for youth groups, young people and youth workers in every activity in the programme*

Sub-group of the Working Party

6.17   There would be considerable value in sharing information with other agencies who employ workers. For example, the Scout Association in the last few years has employed staff for development work and projects in inner city/rural areas throughout the United Kingdom. Guidance and helpful publications are also available from other organisations.

What will the youth worker do?

6.18   The nature and scope of these appointments vary not only in the focus of their work with young people but also in the 'employment' practices taking place. Several full-time youth workers, whether employed by a church or other agency, have expressed concerns.

Concerns of full-time youth workers submitted to the Working Party:

- *There is a lack of clarity regarding their job descriptions (or even the lack of these altogether).*

- *There are unrealistic expectations both of them and the roles/tasks they have been given.*

- *There is uncertainty about continuing funding for their posts and the youth work they are committed to.*

- *There is a need for support and recognition from the whole Church, both locally and nationally.*

- *There is a need for training which equips them to be more effective in their work and which might offer a route(s) to recognised qualifications.*

Sub-group of Working Party

It is clear that issues of recruitment, support, training and recognition of full-time youth workers need to be addressed by the Church at local and national level.

Recruitment

A good, clear written job description includes:

- *an outline of the parish/community*

- *description of other/existing staff functions*

- *statement of main responsibilities and key tasks*

- *personal competencies and qualities looked for in the post holder*

- *terms and conditions of employment*

- *statement regarding equal opportunities policy and practice*

- *statement of support and training to be offered*

6.19   The job description is likely to be the first document received by applicants. It needs to convey a sense of purpose and commitment to the work and to the youth worker, it will also give the applicant an idea about the style and ethos of the church or organisation.

Writing a job description can help the person or group employing the worker to clarify the purpose and the expectations of the job.

Interviews

6.20   The interview is best conducted in a way that seeks information about the candidate, as well as the knowledge, gifts and skills he or she possesses. An interview panel enables several people to comment on the different candidates.

Some people include time with young people in the interview. If this is done as part of an introduction to the building or the area, it also helps the candidate to assess whether the job feels right for her/him.

References

6.21   It is important that the candidate knows the procedures that the church or organisation is following for seeking references. Before sending out information about the job, decisions should be made regarding the number of references, whether they are to be professional or personal, and when they are required.

Offering the job and de-briefing

6.22   It is good practice to make clear to candidates whether the job will be offered immediately following interviews or at a later time. Unsuccessful candidates should be informed as soon as possible. It is also good practice to offer the candidate an opportunity to reflect on the interview in order to identify his or her strengths and weaknesses.

Written confirmation of a job should include:

- *contract of Employment*
- *conditions of service including any polices held by the employer, for example equal opportunity policy and information policy*
- *induction process and probationary requirements*
- *nature of support/training/supervision to be offered (including induction)*
- *details of line management and accountability*
- *date of commencement of employment*
- *who the new employee is to report to in the first instance*
- *details of any specific items the new employee should bring*

Sub-group of Working party

Support

After six months the project had grown from 8 – 80 and with that came its problems! I was on the edge, and about to burn out! The pressure of success and the long hours of work alongside having open house, were beginning to tell on me. There was nowhere I could recharge my batteries and nowhere I could feel support. At the time communication between myself and the rest of the church was poor and this was creating a lot of misunderstanding. I rarely saw my pastor and felt very isolated, a problem that was partly the price of being on the cutting edge, but was also the result of no accountability or relationship with the leaders of the church. In the end my pastor recognised the signs and sent me off for a break. The break had come not a moment too soon!

Leader of a youth project

6.23　It is essential that proper support is given to the youth worker. The church or employer has this obligation not only to the youth worker but through the worker to the young people who are part of the work.

St John's Church Woodbridge, Diocese of St Edmundsbury and Ipswich

Support

In the Contract of Employment we tried to produce a document that not only set out our expectations as employer, but also the kinds of support that we provided for the youth leader. This included professional, clerical and training support. We also wanted to broaden the support base within the church as much as possible. Four particular measures have been taken:

1. *To reconstitute the planning team as the management committee. The committee meets monthly with the youth leader to review the nature and direction of the ministry.*

2. *The Management Committee issues a bi-monthly newsletter to the church and uses all other means to keep the project's profile high. For instance, we have arranged a CPAS/CYPECS speaker for one Sunday.*

3. *A project 'supporter's club' meets monthly for information, sharing and prayer. Any church member can attend, and we have started gathering quite a broad base of support.*

4. *A youth and children's workers' group which is part-social and part-business meets bi-monthly. This might seem an obvious measure, but it has taken the employment of a full-time youth leader to get it functioning properly as part of our overall support strategy and team-building philosophy.*

6.24   As well as formal support for youth workers, informal support is essential. Many Christian workers have a spiritual advisor or director who offer a point of reflection and challenge. Other workers arrange extensive networks of colleagues to provide support and help. Networks exist in each diocese and may operate on parish, deanery or diocesan levels. There are also networks involving the local authority and other agencies. It is important that the youth workers are encouraged to seek involvement in networks which will best support the style and nature of their particular youth work.

Information relating to any person the youth worker is involved with must be treated with respect. Many projects have a policy relating to confidentiality which clearly outlines how, where and when information is disclosed. A policy relating to information sharing supports the worker and indicates a level of respect for those using the project.

6.25   When the youth worker begins employment, an induction process enables him/her to meet other people who have significant roles in the project and generally to get to know how the project operates. It is also a time when other people can welcome the new youth worker and start to network with them.

An induction process for a parish youth worker could include:

- *a welcome to the church, its staff and congregation (a 'commissioning service' may be appropriate)*

- *an opportunity to acquire knowledge of the church's aims, policies and resources*

- *an opportunity to acquire knowledge of wider support/ resources available in the community and from the wider Church*

- *an introduction to health and safety procedures and requirements*

- *the identification of an immediate support person to be referred to*

Sub-group of Working Party

6.26   The expectations in terms of the management, supervision and accountability of the new youth worker have to be clearly stated and understood.

During the induction period it would be helpful to establish an initial pattern for supervision so that the worker knows how and when working matters can be discussed and negotiated and so that she is absolutely sure to whom and for what s/he is responsible.

After induction an ongoing pattern of supervision can be adopted to address the management, training and support of the worker. This will help to keep the work focused and the youth worker resourced and fit.

Training

6.27   A range of opportunities are available in each diocese for youth workers to develop their skills and knowledge in youth work. From submissions to the Working Party it is evident that the need for training is not readily recognised or funded by some parishes. Whether the work is full-time paid, part-time paid or voluntary, youth workers should be offered regular training commensurate with their tasks and duties. Training, whether on site, at college or through residentials, gives experience to the youth worker in a way that will challenge and improve practice.

6.28   It is very important that the church should pay for this training and not expect workers who are already giving time and energy to cope with this expense. 'Fees are an unreasonable cost to restricted family budgets, those on a low wage, etc.' (member of the Working Party). By financing the training the church can be seen to value both the training and the worker.

6.29   Many national organisations such as the uniformed groups, the YMCA/YWCA and other Christian charities have their own programmes for training. Some of these are run on a fairly small scale while others have become fully accredited training programmes which are used by many.

Training with the Church Lads' and Church Girls' Brigade

Successive Annual Reports have made clear that the Brigade is making considerable efforts to ensure that it remains an effective voluntary youth organisation well able to respond to the needs of the modern youngster. From a training perspective this has meant updating and modernising certain existing programmes and the creation of new ones. The emphasis is on development in five principal areas.

1. *Junior Leaders and King George VI Courses*

    Aimed at 16- to 21-year-olds, the Junior Leaders course helps these members grow in confidence and provides a greater opportunity for them to work as leaders. They are introduced to a range of new ideas, skills, experiences and fresh challenges as well as different ways of exploring the Christian faith.

2. *Training Officers*

    In order to improve training generally the Brigade Council has ruled that training officers should be accredited every four years.

3. Leadership Skills Weekends

These are held for each of the four different age groups. The aim is to help the young people to explore new skills and programme ideas. The programme covers a wide range of topics including Christian teaching, games, crafts, drama, safety and programme planning.

5. Taking Groups Away

The Brigade is developing a Leadership Course for leaders in charge of groups. It lays stress on safety and good practice.

Annual Report, 1993-94

The YMCA George Williams College together with the Rank Foundation are jointly involved with well over 50 local projects throughout Great Britain and Northern Ireland. They have developed a unique, five-year, distance learning training programme for professional, informal and community educators as part of the 'Youth or Adult?' initiative. The programme begins at a point equivalent to NVQ/SVQ level 3 and leads to the award of a degree.

There is also the prospect of a part-time youth work qualification at Level 3 (equivalent to A level). This will be delivered through modular programmes of training and development which will be tailored to individual host agencies or employers. There is also work on further enhancing training and support for supervisors and assessors.

The YWCA currently employ 255 full-time and 351 part-time staff. In addition there are approximately 1,000 volunteer committee members and a further 1,000 who assist with the work in one way or another.

Staff training needs are identified through an annual system of appraisal supported by a staff training and development policy. Management training modules for both staff and volunteers are run regularly to cover appraisal, supervision, recruitment and selection, stress and assertiveness. Modules around equal opportunities and team building are planned for 1995.

The YWCA has achieved accreditation as a centre to award Housing NVAs up to Level 4. Future work and training will include exploring the relevance of the RSA scheme of management competencies to local committees and the use of information technology and more detailed knowledge of Housing Corporation requirements.

6.30 Co-operation between these organisations and the Church is widespread and can extend and promote training opportunities for those working with young people. Some organisations welcome the potential of working in partnership with the Church of England and see joint training as one obvious way of working together.

Many Christian agencies have very extensive training programmes which offer opportunities to acquire new skills and knowledge and also network with other workers who are doing the same sort of work. Some youth workers have been able to undertake training offered by Local Education Authorities leading to a recognised qualification as a part-time youth worker.

Full-time youth workers frequently expressed their concerns about the availability of, and access to, training opportunities leading to an accredited qualification. The qualification most widely sought would be recognised both by the Church and by the wider youth service.

Recognition
6.31 Youth workers often feel betrayed by a Church which fails to recognise their ministry. There may be a feeling of isolation and lack of support from their own church but more often it is a desire to be recognised and affirmed by the wider Church.

For those employed full-time as youth workers there is often the additional concern for recognition and a route to qualified status in the eyes of the wider, secular youth service.

Interesting developments in the recognition of youth workers have taken place in the Lutheran Church where youth workers are part of the diaconate. It is important to review this formal recognition in light of youth work practice in the Church of England to assess whether improvements could be made in recognising the important role of youth workers.

Review and evaluation
6.32 Youth work, like any other work, benefits from reviewing the programme, the effect the work is having and evaluating the consequences. This ensures that the work is worthy and of good quality, that the young people involved are getting something out of the venture, and that the conditions of work make the setting a safe place.

An aim in youth work training is to enable youth workers to become 'reflective practitioners', i.e. someone who 'does' youth work but has the ability to reflect on the work's effectiveness and can then improve future work on the basis of this learning experience. Review in this sense is an ongoing process. However, if times are set aside to reflect more on the work over a longer period, different lessons can be learnt. Many projects use the opportunity of their annual general meetings to write a report on the last year's work and to use this information to plan work for the next year. Other project workers use supervision, which may be happening monthly, as a chance to reflect with another experienced worker on their plans and their practice. If aims and objectives are set, then the evaluation process can check whether these have been met, identify any practice which could be improved and channel this thinking into future plans.

Youth work, like any work that is founded on relationships, is difficult to measure and report. It is important that different methods are explored to evaluate creatively the work.

> *Thanet Deanery Youth Project, Kent: How do you Evaluate?*
>
> *Seeking encounters on street corners and providing a friend to young people who are into either truancy, drugs, crime, or just have no alternative but the street corner, is not easy to report. In a region where the causes of the problem are unemployment, homelessness, the general social decline, and often just sheer apathy, the means to prompt the community into financing solutions is equally difficult.*
>
> *This report has been honest in admitting the difficulties of such work but, if financial justification is sought, perhaps the following will set our work into perspective:*
>
> - *at least 5 young people no longer on drugs*
> - *at least 5 young people back in regular schooling*
> - *at least 5 young people deterred from petty crime*
> - *over 80 young people regularly helped*

6.33   The reason that the work is reviewed and evaluated is to fine tune it and make it more effective. The evaluation and review process has a very powerful potential to support and affirm the work as it gives the opportunity for the often implicit aims of the project to be declared and debated. This sharing of aims can help a project to be coherent and can result in the project workers pulling in the same direction.

Resources

6.34   The marginal nature of youth work can be seen in the way that this work is resourced. 'It seems there is great difficulty in encouraging parishes really to allow young people to be actively involved in church life

. . . Parishes are unwilling to spend any money on youth' (response to the Working Party).

> At our church the budget for youth work had been £50 per year. The people who were doing this work found it hard going and generally if youth leaders were needed everyone would keep a low profile so that they were not landed with it. At one meeting the leaders decided that the work with young people had to be improved. As an act of faith the parish allocated the work a budget of £2,000 per year (we did not have this money at the time). The work was also relaunched and people invited to help run the youth work for a limited period only. When this ran out they were under no obligation whatsoever to continue. The effect of the money and this new approach to the work was very energising. Instead of it being the thing that everyone wanted to avoid it became really mainstream and encouraging. Now there are about thirty-five members who come to the youth club and about twenty of them come to church.

> Account of J.D., a young person working in his parish in the
> Diocese of London and member of the Working Party

6.35   In the way that one can look at an industrial company's accounts and deduce the company's priorities, the budget given to youth work gives some indication of how much it is a priority at parish, deanery, diocesan and national levels. One diocesan youth officer asks parishes to compare the amount of money they spend on youth work with the flower budget. Through exercises like this what is revealed is not an encouraging picture. Not only is youth work given a small budget but also the dearth of resources is not limited to money.

> The equipment should be made available to enable every possible opportunity to be taken to communicate with the young people. It is not acceptable for the church youth groups to be dealt the duff equipment that is no longer used by the adult congregation. It is not acceptable for youth groups to be left with the worst worship leaders, the worst musicians and the worst Bible teachers. It is about time the young people were receiving the best that we, the adult church, can give them.

> Youth leader of a church youth group in Kent

6.36   Many curates writing to the Working Party are frustrated at how they are expected to pick up youth work, even with no identified skills in this area.

Curates are often thrust into youth work by their training vicar with a sigh of relief. Frequently the curate is no more suited to the work than his relieved vicar. The relief soon turns to frustration and conflict. Why was no training offered to this curate at theological college? Then no support offered in the job?

Curate with youth work responsibilities

6.37   This need for support and training for those working with young people (both lay workers and clergy) has been echoed in many of the responses to the Working Party for this report. There are Christian organisations working in the country which service their own networks and are available as a resource for parishes. However, the diocesan youth officer has a specific brief to support youth work and in many dioceses is the principal source of professional support. It is unfortunate that this work has been severely threatened by restructuring. In 1988 the number of diocesan youth officers attending their annual conference was over 60; in 1995 there are just over 40 posts and some of these are in long interregnums or have been reduced from full- to half-time. There has been a similar reduction in the national office, with two full-time posts reduced to a full-time and a half-time post. If the work with young people is to be professionally informed, then professionals are needed to resource leaders and the work. The role of diocesan youth officers is to support the network of youth work in the parishes, liaise with other organisations within the diocese and work to resource and improve the quality of youth work in their areas. Many of them also support the ecumenical Spectrum training and hold other training events to improve practice, for example Safe from Harm workshops.

The support given on a diocesan level is much appreciated – this is so essential, a priority.

Curate with youth work responsibilities

6.38   The issue of clergy training is a concern, as the amount of time given to young people's needs on many clergy training courses is minimal. There is also an assumption about the role of the clergy which is geared to working with older members of the congregations within traditional church structures. Concerns have been raised to the Working Party as to whether the expectations of clergy discriminate against different styles of ministry. There may be a role for clergy with specific youth work skills who have undertaken a training which includes youth work options.

Full-time parish youth workers

6.39   There has been a trend recently for a growing number of churches to employ full-time youth workers. These are often churches with an evangelical tradition who see the mission of the Church rooted in their work with young people. This initiative is to be applauded as it is evidence of the Church taking young people seriously. This full-time youth work operates best where youth workers are networked into a system of support and training and can liaise with other youth work initiatives within the deanery and diocese. There are also organisations such as Oasis and Oxford Youth Works which run training and offer support. These networks are crucial, especially when people are employed with a theology that is in accordance with the Church but with no formal youth work training. These courses can provide a good introduction to youth work and enable some of the workers on them to progress to a fully accredited professional qualification. The networks can help with training, help to establish and maintain good practice and help to ensure that health and safety requirements are in place.

Good practice in youth work

6.40   In addition to the areas above which help to safeguard good practice from a professional youth work point of view, structural considerations need to be addressed to ensure that the work is safe and of good quality. Many of these elements are covered in basic youth work training and are the areas addressed when setting up a scheme or project. However in some circumstances where the work with young people has grown up over the years, it is wise to review it. It is helpful if an outside youth worker, a diocesan youth officer or a person with youth work experience can review practice. Guidelines are also available from the county youth service or the diocese to ensure the work is safe, fair and legal.

Planning for good practice

6.41   Youth clubs or youth projects which are planned and reviewed are much more likely to be able to respond in the best way to local needs. Larger projects are often funded only when the funders can be assured that the work is good, safe and well-planned. However, smaller projects also benefit enormously from a simple planning exercise.

> St Andrew's Youth Club, Homfield, Halifax, Diocese of Wakefield
>
> Launched at Easter 1994, after its first year of operation, opening 48
> Sunday evenings with an attendance of 30-45 per night, the follow-
> ing (edited) statement of objectives was produced.

What we are about:

1. We are a Church-based organisation for young people. The St Andrew's PCC fully supports and 'owns' our aims and activities. We are also an affiliated member of the West Yorkshire Youth Association.

2. We reflect the Church's response to God's call to engage with the community, and we are part of its provision for young people. All will be encouraged to be members and no-one will be barred on religious grounds.

3. We aim to cater for those aged 9 and over, living in our parish and the immediate surrounding area. Always subject to the availability of leaders.

4. We aim to understand and respond to the needs of young people, recognising that these will be physical, mental and spiritual.

5. We seek to provide a secure and caring environment in which there will be **respect** for each other, for the aims of the group, and for our buildings and equipment. We reserve the right to bar anyone contravening these basic standards.

6. We provide training and support for our leaders. We also welcome the support of the Diocese, the Youth Association, and we are open to offers of assistance in leadership and in organising activities.

The youth club also produced aims for the short term, the medium term and the long term.

6.42   Many dioceses have produced their own guidelines which are available to help ensure good practice in youth work. There should be help available for projects or churches to draw up policies to ensure good practice. Policies such as equal opportunities or access to information need to be reviewed regularly to ensure that they are being implemented. Every church or project which is working with young people must address these important health, safety and child protection issues to ensure that the youth work is of good quality and that the young people are not made vulnerable by it.

Guidelines will relate to health and safety issues as well as to the Children Act, *Safe from Harm* and child abuse. The broad areas guidelines will address are:

Health and safety

Insurance

Outdoor activities

Equal opportunities

Storage and use of information about young people and workers

Safe from Harm – Child protection

Recruitment, interviewing and support of youth workers

Legislation – Health and Safety

6.43   It cannot be stressed too strongly that any activities run by the Church or Church projects should be safe for young people. Many dioceses have produced their own detailed guidelines which give general rules of good practice whilst also giving specific procedures to follow in the event of an emergency.

Areas which need to be addressed for Health and safety:

- First Aid – adequately trained and identified staff

- Use of drugs or medicines

- Need for expert supervision for activities, e.g. swimming, hill walking, etc.

- Preparation and storage of food

- Information from parents

- Knowledge of fire drill procedure

- Policy on spread of infection – blood fluids

- Supervision – number of adults per group of young people

- Avoidance of adults being alone with young people

- Supervision of sleeping arrangements

- Ensuring privacy for young people

- Transport – should be safe

- Active supervision and policy on use of drugs, alcohol and sexual activity.

- At residentials clear policy and planning on sending people home (for illness or unacceptable behaviour)

- Written delegation of 'loco parentis' to leaders for trips/residentials

- Clear and enforced boundaries about responsibility of leaders (e.g. signing out book if older young people leave a residential)

Legislation – the 1989 Children Act and Safe from Harm

6.44   The following is a summary of recommendations from *Safe from Harm* published by the Home Office (1993)

1. Adopt a policy statement on safeguarding the welfare of children.

2. Plan the work of the organisation so as to minimise situations where the abuse of children may occur.

3. Introduce a system whereby children may talk with an independent person.

4. Apply agreed procedures for protecting children to all paid staff and volunteers.

5. Give all paid staff and volunteers clear roles.

6. Use supervision as a means of protecting children.

7. Treat all would-be paid staff and volunteers as job applicants for any position involving contact with children.

8. Gain at least one reference from a person who has experience of the applicant's paid work or volunteering with children.

9. Explore all applicants' experience of working or contact with children in an interview before appointment.

10. Find out whether an applicant has any conviction for criminal offences against children.

11. Make paid and voluntary appointments conditional on the successful completion of a probationary period.

12. Issue guidelines on how to deal with the disclosure or discovery of abuse.

13. Train staff and volunteers, their line managers or supervisors, and policy makers in the prevention of child abuse.

Small churches or projects may find that many of the recommendations above initially feel cumbersome or difficult. However, without this sort of rigour and commitment to the work with young people we are placing them in a vulnerable position and denying them proper safety in the activities they are involved in.

Insurance

6.45   The young people who are part of the Church's work have a right to be insured against negligence. The youth workers also need protection so that if there is a claim on them they are not held personally responsible. Not only is it unfair to put youth workers in a vulnerable position without adequate insurance but it is also important that their work is seen as part of the wider work of the Church or organisation and is supported in this way.

Many small youth clubs operate using the parish insurance. It is important that this is checked out thoroughly and that confirmation is obtained in writing that all normal activities which are part of the programme are covered by the insurance.

Many dioceses offer an insurance, often in conjunction with a registration scheme, which is specifically designed for the small youth club which runs a range of activities.

Accountability

6.46   Leading a youth work activity can sometimes be quite chaotic. Even if a programme has been fully discussed, planned and organised unforeseen occurrences happen quite frequently. It is essential that there is a very clear line of accountability for all those engaged in the work. A leader running a scheme needs to know who to liaise with if there are any problems.

Clergy involvement in youth work

	Male Clergy	Female Clergy	Total
Sunday School	1,143	328	1,471
CPAS	385	130	515
Children's Clubs	917	136	1,053
Single sex clubs	17	–	17
Mixed Youth Clubs	1,104	147	1,251
Uniformed organisations	532	69	601
Total no of youth work responsibilities	4,098	810	4,908

There are 10–11,000 male clergy and about 1,000 female clergy, nationally.

Statistics: Francis and Lankshear

6.47   From these statistics it can be seen that a very large number of clergy are involved in working directly with young people. An issue which came often to the Working Party was the lament of the curate who was automatically 'given' youth work in the parish as his/her responsibility. A further concern was that there had been no training for this at theological college and the curate felt ill-equipped for tackling this work. Added to this, our stereotypical curate would have little access to any professional or technical support, and no training or training budget to go with this responsibility. Although many of the curates who have been given this work are often pleased to do it, they clearly seek more support in order to do be more effective.

It is interesting to note from the statistics that women clergy are better represented than male clergy proportionally in youth work. About eight hundred jobs are performed by the thousand women clergy compared to just over 4,000 jobs performed by the 10,000 male clergy. Women clergy are thus more than twice as likely to be involved in work with young people than their male colleagues.

Clergy training for youth work

6.48   Responses to the Working Party indicate that many clergy would appreciate youth work training as part of their training for the priesthood. Some feel this is essential. Some training schemes spend a day on youth work, but this is grossly inadequate. Many diocesan youth officers are involved in post-ordination training and are invited into theological colleges on a regular basis. As over a third of the population is under 25 years of age, it is essential for clergy to have some training in this area. This education should include knowledge about the way young people develop and offer some direct work experience where they may acquire skills which will help them to work with young people in the Church and community.

Conclusion

6.49   From the responses submitted to the Working Party it is clear that a vast amount of work is being undertaken by youth workers in various Church and community contexts. The work has become more complex in recent years with the introduction of legislation and the growing awareness about what is good practice within youth work. It is apparent that while many churches and organisations are engaged in ensuring that the work with young people is safe and good, some are operating without addressing these issues. Although young people are working partners within Church and community, there is a responsibility on the part of those in positions of authority and trust to ensure that youth workers are 'safe' people, and the places where youth work happens are 'safe' places. (see paragraph 2.36, section 2) This element of safety and good practice is part of an ongoing tradition of Christian concern and care. The responsibility to ensure this safety and good practice rests on every level of the Church and should be felt and addressed in the parishes, deaneries, dioceses and nationally.

7

Working in Partnership

7.1   In chapter 2 a theology of the Church's work with young people is presented. This theology of youth work is holistic, all encompassing, it is relational, it is within the context of culture, and it is essentially community building. These factors point to positive partnerships both with secular agencies and other Christian agencies, and opportunities to work creatively and promote good youth work both in the Church and in the community (see paragraph 2.3).

Many different agencies work with young people. A sub-group of the Working Party explored the relationship between the Church of England Youth Services (CEYS) and agencies in the same field. The four main areas addressed by the Working Party were the networks established and used by diocesan youth officers, the relationship of the CEYS and local authorities, the work with uniformed organisations and the relationship with YMCA and YWCA.

Partnership networks

Diocesan networks
7.2   Fifty copies of a questionnaire were sent out to the 43 diocesan youth Officers in England or, where vacancies existed, to the respective bishop or director of education. Thirty responses were received, representing just over 67 per cent of the dioceses contacted, or 74 per cent excluding those dioceses without a diocesan youth officer. The results of this questionnaire, analysed below, indicate that professional expertise is clearly valued by a wide range of statutory and voluntary services and committees involved with young people.

Work with voluntary youth councils
Most diocesan youth officers indicated that their work with Local Council of Voluntary Youth Services (LCVYS) is an important and valuable part of their networking activities. Twenty two (73 per cent) of respondents sit on their local committees or councils and in some instances where the diocesan boundaries overlap with more than one local government administrative area, diocesan youth officers sat on two or more LCVYS.

Four diocesan youth officers also sat on larger regional bodies for voluntary youth service.

Comments received in this section:

The Church of England has an important contribution to make to voluntary youth services, but doesn't realise it . . .

Local councils for voluntary youth work are essential in maintaining the trust of voluntary organisation colleagues and in supporting joint training events.

Ecumenical Christian Youth Officers

7.3   Twenty-one of the diocesan youth officers (70 per cent) indicated that a major part of their work is liaising with their fellow diocesan youth officer and youth officers for other Christian denominations, including Frontier Youth Trust and Crusaders.

Our meetings are terribly important for mutual support and have developed many positive partnerships.

Local authority agencies

7.4   Fifteen diocesan youth officers (50 per cent of respondents) revealed that they have regular contact with their local statutory youth/community service. Four indicated regular contacts with social services and schools and five similarly with local health authorities and FE colleges

We have some examples of partnerships but generally the county does its own thing . . .

We have some excellent relations with our county youth service . . .

My salary and training budget are largely funded by the county, but it's a pain trying to categorise Church youth work along county lines!

Police and probation service

7.5   Six diocesan youth officers revealed that they sit on local police liaison committees and/or are involved with probation and youth justice projects.

Uniformed organisations, most notably Scouts and Guides, were cited by eight diocesan youth officers as a regular client group for their time and energy.

Individual personal/professional links

A large number and variety of agencies and organisations were revealed by diocesan youth officers as contributing to their personal and/or professional network. These included:

Local YMCAs (6)	*Princes Trust Committees and/or Projects (3)*
Various Missionary Societies (4)	*National Youth Agency (4)*
Salvation and Church Armies (3)	*Drug/Alcohol Projects (3)*

There were also individual contacts with Childline, Low Pay Unit, Homeless/Housing Project, CYWU, CRE, Rural Development Work, Oasis Trust and Young Farmers.

Analysis of the nature of the personal/professional contacts revealed:

- the majority (19 diocesan youth officers) involved sitting on a committee
- 16 involved either giving (11) or receiving (5) training
- 21 involved either giving (13) or receiving guidance/advice
- 13 involved giving supervision and support
- 9 involved fulfilling a chaplaincy role
- 8 involved delivering a piece of work, e.g. residential or trip, or act of worship.

National Youth Office

7.6   The National Youth Office based at Church House, Westminster, liaises with a large range of organisations. The officers work as part of ecumenical committees such as English Churches Youth Service, Joint Churches Youth Service, and have regular working partnerships with national youth officers from all of the major denominations. One such partnership has been in order to produce the latest edition of Spectrum, the ecumenical part-time training scheme.

The National Youth Office works with the National Council of Voluntary Youth Service and liaises with them and directly with government departments on the formation of policy and law which will affect the work of youth services in the Church. The Youth Office works with organisations such as Time for God an ecumenical scheme to promote young people giving time to volunteer. It is also in regular consultation with schemes such as Greenbelt.

The National Youth Office has an important role in receiving and disseminating information to diocesan youth officers and others in the education network through *Newsboard*, a publication with a circulation of over 500 copies which is published 10 times a year.

The National Youth Office works with young people at Synod, and supports the Young Adult Observation group which has met at York for the last four years. It also provides services for Anglican Youth, an organisation run by young people.

Working with local authorities

7.7   The sub-group decided that an important relationship to explore was the one between the Church of England youth services and local education authorities (or local authorities) who had the statutory responsibility for securing the provision of a youth service in their area. A questionnaire was devised to elicit responses which revealed aspects of this relationship. An invitation was extended to share five factors, points or issued which should be included in the report.

The questionnaire was mailed to 93 local authorities and responses were obtained from 31 or them. The sub-group is extremely grateful to those local authority officers for their efforts in providing responses to the questions. These provide a valuable insight into the characteristics of the relationship at the present time, some of its changes in recent years and some conjectures about likely changes in the immediate future.

7.8   The questions asked and a summary of the responses to them are presented below.

Type of work which local education authorities support
What aid and support do you offer to youth work promoted by the Church of England in your Authority?

Almost all local authorities support youth work provided by the Church of England, characteristically on the same basis as they support other voluntary youth organisations. The norm is for local authorities to have schemes of registration and affiliation for voluntary organisations, either to the local authority or to the local Council of Voluntary Youth Services (CVYS).

The most common areas of support are grant aid towards club and group costs, workers' salaries, and equipment costs; access to county and area events, support of training through access to county provision and/or grant aid for external courses; and discounted fees or free use of educational premises and equipment. One authority mentions funding being available from budgets other than youth service for cultural activities and social services provision.

Advice and support from local authority youth officers, and on occasion from other specialists in the Education Department, appears to be universally available. In some authorities it is specifically focused and channelled through an officer with prime responsibility for liaison with voluntary organisations.

Three authorities indicate that no support is given to the Church of England, because none has been asked for – though they do support uniformed organisations many of which have close connections with a church.

One authority reports reduced support to a diocese because the stop-go nature of their work destroyed local confidence – 'nice people, well intentioned, but they didn't deliver. It simply all faded away'.

Another authority . . .

> . . . does not have contact with the youth work promoted by the Church of England although we have excellent contact with the Methodists... I have never been introduced to the diocesan youth officer – if there is one. I therefore am unable to answer these questions except to say that in general terms 22 per cent of the authority's Youth Service budget goes to Voluntary Youth Organisations.

Aid given to Church youth work
What conditions does this youth work and those who promote it have to fulfil in order to be eligible and qualify for your aid and support?

Are there any kinds of youth work that it is appropriate for the Church of England to promote that you find or would find inappropriate to support?

All authorities have a range of general and threshold conditions which they require registered and affiliated organisations to meet. These include such basic indicators of accountability as a management committee and audited accounts. Some require organisations to be established and stable. Others will provide start-up grants. All specify an age range beyond which work will not be supported. The range at its greatest extreme is from 5 to 25, and at its most restrictive from 13 to 19.

The need for voluntary organisations to have equal opportunities policies and/or practices to comply with the local authority's own policies is explicitly stated in most cases.

One local authority gives priority to work by voluntary organisations which the professional officers would want to provide but which they are prevented from doing by the political considerations of local authority members. Others echo the curriculum priorities indicated in DFE policy statements.

Only two authorities claim that there is no kind of youth work that they could not support. The major criteria for excluding work from support are closed membership of the group and the intention of evangelism. One expresses it as the 'impossibility of supporting work involving the development of young people within a wholly Christian fellowship or an activity which is primarily about the development of Christian doctrine and youth worship'. Another indicates the exclusion of 'work restricted to Christians or work which actually promotes Christian belief'.

One respondent comments that any work is eligible, but no applications have been received from Church of England groups within the last five years. Another indicates that out of the 450 registered groups, only 6 are Church of England, whilst many more are Methodist.

Changing patterns of support over time

Is your aid and support for youth work promoted by the Church of England on the same basis and under the same conditions as your aid and support to youth work provided by:

a)   **other voluntary youth organisations;**

b)   **other Christian churches and agencies;**

c)   **the agencies of other faiths?**

This question secured the greatest unanimity of all the questions asked. All respondents indicated 'yes' to each of the three sub-questions. One indicated that though the basis of and conditions for aid and support were the same, in practice they could lead to different outcomes and reported that the Church of England received grant aid, the Roman Catholics a specific appointment and Muslims, Sikhs and Hindus received support for part-time workers.

One respondent indicated that within this equality framework differential criteria could be applied: 'we remain watchful of any group who may be considered as a "cult" and similarly with certain aspects of charismatic worship (where physical contact is encouraged).'

Church work supported by Local Education Authorities

In what ways, if any, is your aid and support, and the conditions that have to be fulfilled for it to be given, different now from what it was in the recent past (e.g. at other times during the last decade)?

What further changes, if any, do you envisage in your aid and support, and the conditions that have to be fulfilled for it to be given, in the not too distant future (e.g. during the next few years)?

Very few authorities report no change in both the conditions or the levels of aid. Nearly all have reduced the level of aid and support and, more significantly, the conditions under which it is made available.

The changes in the conditions are all in the direction of requiring voluntary provision to be targeted to meet specific criteria and to be evaluated for effectiveness. There are often specifications of priority groups and purposes; the most common being to provide services in the areas of disadvantage and poverty and to provide equal opportunities. These moves lead to payments being linked for sessions of work delivered rather than payments for organisational costs. The changes in the conditions are far-reaching. Work must deliver the key priorities of the local authority or those agreed by them, usually through a CVYS. Work is more tightly monitored, with a greater requirement of accountability. These arrangements are increasingly being formalised in service level agreements. One authority indicates that the provision of voluntary organisations is 'inspected'.

A small number of authorities report that no change in the present arrangements is anticipated, though of these some indicate that uncertainties make the question difficult to answer. Among those who envisage no change, there are some who acknowledge that increasing financial stringency may well require a review of their purposes and procedures for the aid and support of voluntary organisations.

The vast majority envisage change, and of these the greater number indicate further application of requirements to secure local authority priorities and to meet specific targets. One authority is this year beginning a phased introduction of the requirements for voluntary organisations to prepare and submit business plans before aid and support will be considered. One authority expects services to merge and to work more collaboratively through the local CVYS. Another indicates that joint Local Authority/Voluntary Sector planning will operate at the local level with a consequent withdrawal of funding for those who choose not to be involved.

Church of England's support of LEA work
Are you aware of any aid and support given to youth work promoted by the Church of England by other departments of your local authority or any of the minor authorities within your local authority area?

Nineteen of the 31 local authorities who responded to this question indicated that they were unaware of any grant aid or support given by other departments in their authorities or by minor authorities in their local authority area to youth work in the Church of England.

Of the few who were aware that the Church of England in their area received such aid and support, the majority indicated that this was provided by social services, the careers service and health promotion and economic development units. Two authorities mentioned initiatives promoted by the library service. One authority also mentioned some cross-funding between schools and voluntary organisations. Support from district and other minor authorities was described as patchy geographically and *ad hoc* rather than continuous.

Partnership working within the curriculum
Does the Church of England contribute to your provision of a Youth Service?

Though there were 8 responses that indicated no contribution of the Church of England other than the Church's provision of youth groups and clubs, other responses indicated a number of contributions. These appear to be much appreciated.

Foremost among these were diocesan contributions to – and often leadership with – the local CVYS, and within local authority committees and working parties. Contributions to joint training programmes were frequently mentioned. A Church of England contribution to special events and to multi-agency projects was also much appreciated. Mention was frequently made, however, of the recent curtailment of these functions because of the staffing cuts in youth officer provision by dioceses.

Church action in providing liturgical events and celebrations was also mentioned.

A greater availability of the Church of England, not merely to the local authority, but to other voluntary organisations, was emphasised as desirable in one response. Another response, however, indicated that the Church's image of young people in the 1990s was derived from the 1970s, and that it failed to provide for the 15+ group. Another authority reported that 'where the contact is good there is a very effective relationship', but went on to say that 'the major problem is the lack of an obvious network with Church of England youth work'. Another response commented that there is scope for greater co-operation between the diocesan youth service and the local authority youth service and that an annual plan for co-operative projects would be helpful. Four respondents indicated that the Church could make a greater contribution to the development of policies and practice within the youth service curriculum for spiritual development. Of the many responses that indicate substantial contributions from diocesan personnel and occasionally field workers to training programmes, one indicates little support for county training events from Church of England voluntary workers.

> The Diocesan Officer doesn't really contribute to the statutory service in any meaningful way – possibly because of time restrictions or job demands on one person . . . Discussions have been held in the past on joint training initiatives, etc. but do not seem to have resulted in Church of England youth workers participating in any programmes. There also appears to be little or no involvement in county or area events which are a big feature of (our) Youth Service. Many more young people could benefit from the county facilities and resources which are open to them – but despite receiving information – participation is minimal from Church groups.

Curriculum provision
What five points, factors or issues should be in the report?

The curriculum of youth work in the Church was raised, the concerns with this area are as follows:

- There is a need for the Church to make clear statements about its objectives in youth work and of the value to young people of what it delivers.

- Those objectives can include contributions to evangelism and the lives of young Christians, especially in helping them to find roles and activities for themselves within the Church and helping the Church to create access and space for them.

- By far the largest number of comments indicated a concern that the Church in any place should not limit its youth service to those it wished to evangelise or those who were already members. The greatest stress was laid on:

  - targeting and developing work with the disadvantaged and those who are vulnerable and at risk so that oppression and discrimination are challenged and lessened; and

- developing a curriculum that enables young people to develop the skills for living in society and coping with such issues as drugs, health, sexuality and economic and social deprivation within a framework that would develop equal opportunities and empower them in society.

- The churches in rural areas should play a vital role in providing a youth service for all the young people who live there. Within that service they should address those particular needs of young people that are derived from living in rural areas.

- The Church should help develop a youth work curriculum for spiritual development which is applicable to and can be adopted by any young persons, and not just by those who are committed Christians. It should make available to other youth organisations its insights into such experiences as young people and bereavement, the nature of conscience and the development of values.

- In multi-faith areas the Church is in a unique position to accept responsibility for enabling young people of different faiths to relate to each other to promote understanding and celebrate differences.

An educational officer of one local authority cites with evident approval that:

> An incarnational view of the Church underlines diocesan youth service policy.

> It is assumed that whilst an awareness of the ultimate significance of personal faith and the truth of the Christian gospel underlines youth work policy, the criteria for success in this area of work will not simply amount to youthful bottoms on pews.

> The second assumption is a prophetic view of (the relationship of) the Church and society. It is assumed that the Church's prophetic role in society is to identify areas of concern which inhibit the fulfilment of potential (for example: alcohol, drugs, immigration regulations, unemployment, homelessness); to explore ways in which these concerns might be addressed and to initiate schemes to do so.

Partnership

7.9   The concerns within this area are as follows:

- full partnership requires a full-time diocesan youth officer in order to establish and maintain full relationships with full-time local authority colleagues and full-time colleagues in voluntary organisations.

- how the roles of diocesan youth officers and bishop's youth chaplains can give a greater emphasis to the fostering of collaboration and partnership with the local authorities and other voluntary youth organisation.

- the need for joint or co-operative planning and deployment of services is increasingly essential as resources diminish. Pointers should be given about how the Church at diocesan and parish levels can work jointly or co-operatively with other Church agencies. It is important for partnership to exist at all levels from that of policy-making to the operational.

- The church, especially at local level, should be made aware of and encouraged to take up both

  - the range of aid and support available to it from the local authority; and

  - the range of opportunities for the young people in its youth groups to participate in events and activities with young people from other groups and clubs.

Conclusion

7.10   The overall impression from these responses is of a Church whose contribution is welcomed, appreciated and valued when it is made, and regretted when it is either not made or falls short. There was sadness rather than recrimination in those three local authorities in which the Church of England had proved incapable or unwilling to contribute to the development of the Youth Service.

7.11   The contribution of the Church is not only in the direct provision that it makes for young people. It is also in the significant contributions that it makes to the development and delivery of policy and curriculum. It plays a particularly valuable and often crucial role in the arena of voluntary youth organisation co-operation and collaboration.

7.12   It should be remembered that the responsibility of local authorities 'to secure the provision' of a youth service provision has been a constant and on going activity since the ending of the World War II. To opt out of it or to lessen the priority and status given to 'partnership' would not only irreparably damage the Youth Service in this country but would damage the Church.

This exercise in listening to the local authorities has pointed out the need for the Church to be committed to and acting in partnership with the local authorities and with other voluntary youth organisations. There is a need for this role to be exercised at diocesan level, for the local authorities have a responsibility for researching need and planning and securing a youth service in their areas as well as developing policies that are more effective and efficient. But there is much more of a need for the local Church in deanery and parish to aim to provide the kind of service to young people that these responses have indicated is increasingly needed.

Working with uniformed organisations

7.13   Many uniformed organisations meet on church premises and work in partnership with Anglican churches. Sometimes this partnership is extensive with church members and clergy working as leaders within the uniformed organisations, sometimes the relationship is more distinct and separate. In any case 152,914 young people attend uniformed organisations which are linked in some way to the Church of England and with them are 9,440 young people with leadership responsibilities.

This represents a substantial contact with young people and is a link which can be fostered and used. Many of the uniformed organisations wrote to say how they would appreciate a more active involvement of the Church. Where these opportunities of working in partnership have been taken they are very creative and worthwhile for both parties.

Scouts and Guides

7.14   There are over one and a half million Scouts and Guides in the United Kingdom, and they are part of a much larger international movement. This number reflects the excellent work done with younger Scouts and Guides; Beavers, Cubs, Rainbow Guides and Brownies, as well as the older members: Scouts, Venture Scouts, Guides and Ranger Guides. Francis and Lankshear's survey shows that 66,219 Scouts (10-25 years) and 70,815 Guides (10-25 years) are connected to Anglican Churches.

The National Scout Chaplain, Canon Mark Bryant, points out that 'the Church is concerned about young people – and very many young people are not in the churches. Many young people are in Scouting and Guiding. The Church would do well to see how it can improve its relationships with this large number of people'. This improved relationship would, according to the chaplain, have other positive benefits. 'It would however be a great mistake to see engagement with Scouting and Guiding as simply being about youth work. There are a large number of adults involved in Scouting and Guiding who are not in our Churches. Many of them are people with a deep commitment to values, to helping other people and to creating a better community. The Church can usefully engage with such men and women of good will.

7.15   Canon Mark Bryant also identifies the Scout or Guide chaplain as an interpreter, linking the Church to the Scouts and Guides and vice versa. He says that 'both Church and Scouting have significant public relations difficulties. In the community, the perception of Scouting and of the Church belies the very good and creative work which both are often undertaking. The chaplain can be a bridge between these two organisations'.

> I suspect that a large number of Scout leaders have links with their local churches. Local churches should seek to encourage and affirm Scout leaders in what they are doing, irrespective of whether or not they are working with a sponsored group. In this, as in other areas, local churches must beware of putting too much pressure on lay people to become involved in specifically church-based activities.
>
> In a number of areas, not least in Urban Priority Areas, Scouting and Guiding is having to close down for lack of leaders. It may well be right to challenge Christians to consider whether they should go and engage in youth work with Scouts and Guides, in communities where such youth work is often most greatly needed.
>
> Canon Mark Bryant, National Chaplain to the Church of England Scouts

7.16   The Executive Committee of the Anglican Fellowship of Scouts and Guides responded to the report and wrote of how the Church should include young people and that they should be integrated into the life of the Church.

Both Guiding and Scouting are open to all faiths and each member has 'to promise to do their best to do their duty to God'. Scouting aims to take account of the different religious obligations of its members while upholding the essential spirit of the promise. 'In the phrase to love God or duty to God the word God can be replaced by Allah, my Dharma or others as appropriate' (from Scouts Guides and the Church, Southwark Diocesan Board of Education). At a recent training day Canon Bryant said 'Scouting differentiates clearly between spiritual and religious development. Increasingly, the Association is looking to the denominations to provide religious development for those who have relationships with their local faith communities. This is a clear area where Scouting is looking for support from the local churches, and it is clear that the Chief Scout is considerably committed to this. In my opinion the Churches would be foolish to ignore this opportunity.' He also says that many leaders may be anxious about the whole area of spiritual development and that there is a role for ministers who can win the confidence of these leaders and help them to understand what this is about.

Guidelines for good practice between Scouts, Guides and the Church
What the clergy and the parish can do:

- meet the leaders
- know the Promise and Law
- join in an event
- offer your skills, e.g. for badge work and activities
- get to know the local Commissioners
- note the dates of major events
- remind the Scouts/Guides of the Church's seasons
- visit a camp or indoor activity
- meet parents of Scouts/Guides
- be aware of the resources Scouting/Guiding need
- provide or help find a place to meet at a reasonable cost
- know something about Scouting/Guiding in the District
- encourage Venture Scouts/Ranger Guides to join a church community
- be aware of opportunities to encourage young people and their families to join the life of the Church

What the Scouts and Guides can do:

- support church services and the work of the Sunday School
- get involved in the planning of services when appropriate
- participate in the life of the youth programme of the church
- liaise with clergy on dates of events
- encourage membership of the Parochial Church Council by those qualified to seek elections
- appoint a Scout Group Chaplain
- act as sidespersons, servers, choir, bell ringers
- lead prayers or read a lesson
- act as hosts at a reception to mark a festival
- help with church fundraising events and social occasions
- entertain clergy to a patrol activity, e.g. dinner
- report to the Parochial Church Council regularly
- ask the congregation for their help

From Scouts, Guides and the Church, Southwark Diocesan Board of Education

Boys' Brigade and Girls' Brigade

7.17 The first Boy's Brigade company was formed in 1883 in Glasgow as part of the local Mission Extension for the Sunday School lads of the Free College Church. Since then the movement has grown, joined with The Boys' Life Brigade and was a forerunner of the uniformed youth organisations. The object of the Boys Brigade is 'the advancement of Christ's Kingdom among boys and the promotions of habits of Obedience, Reverence, Discipline, Self-respect and all that tends towards a true Christian Manliness'. The Brigade's purpose is worked out in individual companies operating within their churches to present the Christian message to boys and young men. There is a strong tradition of music in the Brigade.

The Girls' Brigade with the commission 'Seek Serve and Follow Christ' works with many girls and young women in England, Great Britain and overseas. There are many opportunities given to Girls' Brigade members to take part in a range of activities and experiences with others which will help develop all aspects of their lives. This is expressed in a letter to the Girls' Brigade Gazette where a company lieutenant writes to 'express our profound desire to see the Girls' Brigade grow and flourish in the coming years and through it to see girls owning Jesus as their Saviour and Lord'.

> *Boys' Brigade and Girls' Brigade*
>
> *There are 4,318 boys (10-25 years) attending Boys' Brigade Companies in Anglican Churches.*
>
> *There are 1,244 girls (10-25 years) attending Girls' Brigade Companies in Anglican Churches.*
>
> Statistics: Francis and Lankshear

Church Lads' and Church Girls' Brigade

7.18 In 1994 the Church Lads' and Church Girls' Brigade had a membership of 8,633. Fifty five per cent of the group are male and forty five per cent female. The number of young people between 10 and 25 years were 2,889 (Francis and Lankshear). The Brigade has for an object 'to extend the Kingdom of Christ among lads and girls and to encourage faithful membership of the Church of England or other episcopal Churches in communion with the Church of England by bringing them together in groups organised for religious, educational and recreational activities'. The Brigade has a strong musical tradition, with a national choir and local choirs, and a national band as well as local bands. There is a strong emphasis on training and bringing young people into leadership roles.

Other uniformed agencies

7.19   There are other uniformed agencies which are connected with Anglican Churches. Francis and Lankshear's figures shows 707 young women who are members of the Girls' Friendly Society, which is sometimes uniformed, and 3,215 young women (10–25 years) belonging to other uniformed organisations. The figure for young men is 2,228 (10–25 years). These organisations include the Woodcraft Folk, St John's Ambulance and Red Cross.

Conclusion

7.20   Many uniformed organisations working with young people are engaged with Christian work. The range of this work includes organisations that work with people from all religions and see faith development as a crucial element in a young person's life. It also includes work which has a specific and explicit Christian focus. The relationship that these uniformed organisations have with their local churches is mixed. Some partnerships work extremely well and there is a mutual agenda and understanding. However, in some circumstances the uniformed organisations do not have a good relationship and the church acts simply as a venue for the meetings.

The number of young people who are reached by these agencies is considerable, and some of these young people have little or no knowledge of the Church. Faith and worship is a significant element of the work of many of the uniformed organisations. There are possibilities of creative mutual work and it is important both for the Church and for the organisations to realise the huge potential of partnership.

Working with other agencies and networks

YMCA *and* YWCA

7.21   The Young Men's Christian Association (YMCA) and the Young Women's Christian Association of Great Britain (YWCA) are membership movements which are open to all young people. There is a contact at the national level through links with the broader ecumenical grouping of Churches Together in England and the Council for Churches in Britain and Ireland. There are also local and diocesan links where both representatives of the church and the YMCA and YWCA sit on boards and committees. A number of bishops are YMCA presidents and at local level some YWCA units have more closely defined relationships with local parishes. Locally some clergy play a chaplain's role in YMCAs.

While good working relationships were valued there is a tension in any ecumenical organisation in wanting to increase working relationships with other agencies and churches whilst not wanting to particularly favour one denomination.

> *The YMCA is non-denominational and therefore needs to be involved only in appropriate structural relationships which recognise this.*
>
> YMCA response to the Working Party

7.22   The YWCA seeks to strengthen relationships with Churches through the broader ecumenical meetings. The YMCA suggested that to improve the relationship with the Church of England there could be a regular exchange of information, that individuals in the Church could be used as consultants for YMCA projects and YMCA could provide consultancy for the Church. There is also the opportunity of joint funding of projects, and allocation of Church Urban Fund money to YMCA projects.

The YMCA also suggested that there were opportunities for joint work with young people particularly in Urban Priority Areas and the possibility of sharing youth work training.

The YMCA reported that relationships with senior managers and diocesan youth officers worked well and local projects which were organised jointly at parish or diocesan level were successful. An example cited was the Portsmouth YMCA/Diocesan Bus Project.

Christian faith is encouraged in different ways. The YMCA encourage Christian faith 'by service, example to the seeker, and by different programmes such as tensing and discussion groups'. Within the YMCA there are study groups, individual support and an encouragement to participate in a local church. An annual camp, Eurocross, is also organised, where through epilogues, etc., young people are involved in worship. One of the aims of the YWCA is 'to promote opportunities for exploration of the Christian faith and for wider spiritual support'. This aim is part of a broad spiritual approach.

> *As a membership movement which is open to all, we encourage Christian faith within the wider context of an awareness of spiritual needs of the young women who form our members and participants and encouragement to them to pursue exploration of these needs which might lead them to ask questions about the Christian faith or might lead them in other directions. This relationship is an integral part of many YWCA activities and the extent to which this takes place within the context of any youth group will vary enormously at local units around the country.*
>
> YWCA, letter to the Working Party

7.23   Whilst wanting to keep the ecumenical nature of the organisations, both the YMCA and the YWCA welcome work with the Church of England. The lack of named contacts, and mutual knowledge of procedures and structures is something that the YMCA suggests inhibits greater partnership. Also at a local level sometimes their relationships are not effective.

The successful working relationships and projects indicate what can be done when good partnerships exist. As with the uniformed organisations there is a great potential in increasing working partnerships and these can offer the YMCA, the YWCA and the Church of England tremendous possibilities to extend their work.

WORKING WITH NATIONAL ORGANISATIONS

7.24   A large number of organisations operate nationally and locally. Some of these organisations have specific Christian educational or missionary aims, others offer a general youth work programme which incorporates and encourages spiritual development. It is difficult to represent all these organisations and the Working Party acknowledge a massive investment of time, energy and commitment through these works. Examples of some of these organisations are in paragraph 3.16.

Crusaders

Crusaders is an inter-denominational youth organisation helping churches and Christians reach young people with the love of Jesus through youth groups, holiday programmes and special events. The emphasis is on relevance and on equipping volunteers with leadership training, active teaching materials and the latest specialist youth resources through local and national support. Full-time area development workers can visit groups of churches to give presentations as to how best to reach unchurched young people and the resources available. Crusaders has been experiencing its fastest ever rate of growth in the last five years.

The movement is committed to cutting edge youth work and has undergone radical changes to this end. Recent work includes publishing Fast Moving Currents in Youth Culture and an outreach project to disadvantaged young people in rural and urban priority areas. A recent road show reached over 6,000 young people and over 1,500 made a commitment to Christ. Crusaders work continues with the establishment of an Advisory Council and a fresh emphasis on spiritual priorities especially prayer.

Letter from Olaf Fogwill to the Working Party

Ecumenical work

7.25   Diocesan youth officers regularly link with other Christian denominations and with liaise with them for a significant part of their work. The national youth officers work with their counterparts from other denominations on specific projects, e.g. Spectrum training, and national events, e.g., the 'Roots and Wings' conference in Glasgow 1996 for youth workers. The national ecumenical organisations such as YMCA, YWCA, Christian Aid, etc. give opportunities of working in partnership with other denominations. There are a large number of small local projects which are funded and supported by more than one denomination.

> *On The Edge Bus Project, Diocese of Truro*
>
> *The* On The Edge *project, run by Steve and Lin Bedford, is based in Tiverton, Devon. The double decker bus is used on two evenings every week as part of the ongoing outreach to local young people. The team includes three or four young people who join the team for a year as volunteers. The main thrust of the work is to reach young people who in reality have no interest in Christianity, and would never have contact with Christians in their local area. In Wellington and Tiverton where we work regularly with the bus, we are helped by Christians of all denominations from local churches who are committed to the bus ministry and see it as a bridge between the Church and young people who we meet on the streets. Relationships are built between Christians and the young people which ultimately provide a basis for a positive witness and conversations about their own beliefs.*

There is also much co-operation in planning and running large events such as Rave in the Nave (see paragraph 4.17). The Spectrum part-time youth worker training scheme is written and delivered ecumenically (see paragraph 6.4).

Interfaith work

> *On 19 July 1995 at Lambeth Palace the Archbishop of Canterbury met twenty-five 16- to 18-year-olds of different faiths and ethnic backgrounds from schools around Britain. Participants representing all of Britain's nine major faiths (Baha'i, Buddhist, Christian, Hindu, Jain, Jewish, Muslim, Sikh and Zoroastrian) came from all over England to promote the 'All Different, All Equal' Youth Campaign.*
>
> *The Archbishop of Canterbury said 'In many places around the world, conflict between faiths is a sad reality. We must hope that it never comes to divide our country. Young people have a special role to*

play in building bridges of inter faith friendship and understanding.
They hold our future in their hands.

7.26   Although many churches are in multi-faith and multi-culture areas there was not very much contact reported with Church of England youth services and youth officers of other faiths. One reason given for this was that this work is under-resourced. However, there are small but encouraging initiatives in various parts of the country where individuals seek to make links with others from different faiths. An example is that of the youth officer from the Diocese of Liverpool who has worked with a Muslim youth worker to adapt the Spectrum part-time youth work training scheme so that it can be used for training workers who are Muslim.

Nationally the Buddhists at Holy Island have various ecological projects which are run on an interfaith basis and scholarships have been extended to encourage young people from the Church of England to take part.

There is also an Interfaith Network which has organised a day to discuss interfaith initiatives with young people and acknowledges that the work currently is isolated and restricted to individual efforts. They have produced some guidelines which help to encourage and strengthen relationships between faiths while acknowledging the difference between religions and ensuring that the identity of each faith is retained and respected (see paragraph 2.36, section 3).

The 'code of conduct' for interfaith relations begins:

In Britain today, people of many different faiths and beliefs live side by side. The opportunity lies before us to work together to build a society rooted in the values we treasure. But this society can only be built on a sure foundation of mutual respect, openness and trust. This means finding ways to live our lives of faith with integrity, and allowing others to do so too. Our different religious traditions offer us many resources for this and teach us the importance of good relationships characterised by honesty, compassion and generosity of spirit.

It ends:

Living and working together is not always easy. Religion harnesses deep emotions which can sometimes take destructive forms. Where this happens, we must draw on our faith to bring about reconciliation and understanding. The truest fruits of religion are healing and positive. We have a great deal to learn from one another which can enrich us without undermining our identities. Together, listening and responding with openness and respect, we can move forward to work in ways that acknowledge genuine differences but build on shared hopes and values.

Conclusion

7.27   The Church of England works with a large number of other agencies in both Christian, other faiths and secular fields. Very exciting and innovative initiatives have emerged from joint working and partnerships with other agencies and organisations. However, many of the agencies that responded to the Working Party reflected that the full potential of partnership was not being reached and that they would welcome better links and opportunities for joint working. If the Church wants to engage in this work it is important that it organises the internal resources to do so. A single diocesan youth officer working over a large diocese can only have an effective working relationship with a very few people. If youth workers working locally have sufficient resources then examples of good practice can be spread and used to encourage others. Nationally, coordinating work takes time and resources, and with only one and a half national youth officers work is necessarily limited. When resources are limited the partnership and outreach work is usually the first work to go or be minimised. However, what is apparent is how effective the Church has been in making relationships and partnerships within youth work, given the limited resources available. It is important to see that with increased resources this work could be considerably expanded and to realise that for youth work to be relational our contact with other agencies must be relational.

8

The Church's Role – Past, Present and Future

8.1   The Church of England has had a significant impact on youth work in England. As an organisation it has worked in partnership with statutory services towards better youth work. It has also worked through thousands of parishes at providing opportunities for young people. Many thousands of committed Christian men and women who have worked both in the voluntary and statutory sectors to create and sustain good quality youth work.

This chapter starts with an outline of the historical background of youth work and the Church's involvement in this. This section takes us up to the present time. The next section looks from the present, which has been outlined in the body of this report, to the future and explores some of the key ways in which the Church can engage with youth work in the wider society.

Perspectives from past work

The Youth Service in England
8.2   The 'youth service' in England developed in the late nineteenth century. The earliest voluntary youth organisations were started by philanthropic individuals, many of whom were Christian. The Young Men's Christian Association (YMCA) and the Girls' Friendly Society are amongst those which aimed to provide education and leisure opportunities for young workers. In the second half of the century charity work on behalf of working young people mushroomed and was led by city centre evangelical missions and ragged schools where clubs for young people began to be formed. In 1884 there were 300 institutes and working boys clubs in the Diocese of London alone and most of these were associated with churches.

Work this century up to 1944
8.3   Between 1900 and 1960 there was a remarkable growth in voluntary youth work agencies. National structures within the Church of England were created to debate and consider youth work issues and in

1938 the Central Youth Council of the Church of England was formed. This became the Church of England Youth Council (CEYC) in 1942. The voluntary organisations which served young people were drawn together in 1936 to form the Standing Conference of Juvenile Organisations, which was later to become the Standing Conference of National Youth Organisations.

In 1939 a government circular entitled 'In Service of Youth' enabled the State to give money to support voluntary organisations in providing a youth service for 14- to 21-year-olds. This circular pointed out the need to work with girls and advocated that young people should be part of the decision making processes of their organisations.

1944 *onwards*

8.4   The 1944 Education Act endorsed this circular and laid the foundations for the future statutory youth service.

In 1951 Lord Redcliffe-Maud, Permanent Secretary of the Ministry of Education, defined the aim of youth services as:

> *to offer individual young people in their leisure time, opportunities of various kinds, complementary to those of home, formal education and work, to discover and develop their personal resources of body in mind and spirit and thus better equip themselves to live the life of mature creative and responsible members of the Free Society.*

8.5   A significant report, The Albermarle Report – The Youth Service in England and Wales (1960) proposed:

● *the establishment of a Youth Service Development Council at National Level*

● *training for full-time youth leaders to overcome projected shortages (at the time there were estimated to be 700 full-time youth leaders).*

● *more money for local authorities, in particular to provide purpose-built youth centres.*

The government welcomed this report and committed itself to implementing the recommendations. Immediate action was taken and £28 million was made available to fund a building programme and to increase the number of full-time youth workers from 700 to 1800.

Further reports included:

● 1962 – The Bessie Report focussed on training part-time youth leaders and assistants. This formed the basis of both voluntary and statutory part-time youth work training.

- 1969 – Youth and Community Work in the 1970s – Proposals by the Youth Service Development Council – known as the Milson-Fairbairn Report, argued for the youth service to adopt a community development approach, and suggested that it had a crucial role in creating 'active' society. The report stated 'its concern to help young people to create their place in a changing society and it is their critical involvement which is the goal'.

- 1982 – Experience and Participation – Report of the Review Group on the Youth Service to the Secretary of State for Education and Science – also known as the Thompson Report clearly stated that the prime objective of the youth service was personal development of the individual through reflection on experience.

Most recent developments

8.6   In the late 1980s and 1990s, Ministerial conferences have been the main governmental instrument for changing policy. Through these a mission statement for the youth service and the youth work curriculum has evolved.

Within all the developments resulting from the national reports above, covering the past 35 years, it is important to note that the Church of England, at local, regional and national level, has played a significant role by supporting, contributing to and, in many instances, pioneering a wide range of youth work initiatives. Notable among these pioneering aspects which influenced subsequent statutory provision have been the numerous city centre-based detached youth projects; coffee bar advice and coun-selling shops; work with the transient and homeless; night-shelters for the young; hostel accommodation schemes for unmarried young mothers; motor car and bike projects; and innovative schemes of training for part-time youth workers. These initiatives have been an active expression of the Church's concern for the Christian nurture of young people and a desire to engage with issues that impinge on the lives of young people in the com-munity.

Successive government reports and a number of Private Members' Bills have pressed for local education authorities to be legally required to provide a youth service, but this has not been achieved. Youth service funding is marginalised when local government budgets are drawn up. Recently in the light of local authority cutbacks, funding for the statutory and voluntary youth service has been substantially reduced.

The struggle to build and sustain relationships with individual young people and community groups becomes even greater when projects are faced with short-term funding and uncertainties about ongoing financial support.

In 1994 the Sufficiency Working Group published a consultative paper, which continues to advocate the need for 'an adequate and sufficient' youth service.

The Church of England Youth Council

8.7   In the 1960s and 1970s the Church of England Youth Council (CEYC) enabled the Church of England to contribute to the development of the youth service. CEYC was recognised by the government as one of the largest elements of the youth service. The CEYC also drew its membership from other denominations as well as the Church of England itself and was a key initiator of policy and thinking in youth work at this time.

During the 1960s the Church of England Youth Council was often at the leading edge of youth service developments particularly in the following areas:

● the study of school based youth and community work

● establishing a drug advisory group

● coordinating international visits for youth workers (to the USSR and Germany)

● conducting a survey of Church of England Youth Centres

● producing a report on work with under 14s

● encouraging, supporting and sustaining youth work at a parochial level.

In the field of training the CEYC was the first to offer a programme of 'training the trainer', initiated in an inter-professional in-service training programme, and coordinated the first conference of diocesan youth chaplains/officers.

During this period the CEYC also focused on:

● post-confirmation training for young people

● participation of young people in the decision making processes of the Church

● establishing a number of residential centres for youth work

● publishing numerous reports and papers on specific aspects of youth work.

In its programme for young people the CEYC offered a national youth week end in which the Archbishop of Canterbury preached in Westminster Abbey and hosted between 1,500 and 2,000 young people at Lambeth Palace. There was also a youth conference at Butlins, Minehead, attended by 1,000 15- to 21-year-olds.

The above work, undertaken on behalf of the Board of Education, would not have been achieved without those staff appointed to national youth officer posts taking responsibility for these and other initiatives, including the support, training and development of the diocesan youth officer network.

The emergence and development of the Diocesan Youth Officer's role

8.8   Early in its existence the Church of England Youth Council advocated that each of the 43 dioceses of the Church of England should have a full-time diocesan officer. By 1969, eighty diocesan youth officers were in post, 38 of them full-time. Often appointed as chaplains, the diocesan youth officer's role was to:

●   support and encourage work with young people in parishes

●   provide training for youth leaders/workers

●   integrate the Church's work with young people into the wider youth service and liaise with other youth organisations

●   provide and organise events for young people to complement those offered at parish and deanery level.

The detailed job descriptions of each diocesan youth officer vary from diocese to diocese and reflect the independent nature of the diocesan structure.

8.9   The growing professionalism of the youth service led dioceses to appoint personnel with appropriate and specific training in youth and community work into the key role of diocesan youth officer. As a consequence, during the 1970s and early 1980s the diocesan youth officer network began to reflect this in the ever increasing number of lay people being appointed to these posts with youth work qualifications and experience. This change in appointment practice was influenced by the need to honour the calling of ordained people to the parochial ministry rather than specialist ministries that could be more readily undertaken by appropriately qualified and trained lay people. Another influence may well have been the impact of part or full funding of posts by the local education authority and the requirements they stipulated. By the end of the 1980s a significant number of diocesan youth officers were lay people (some female) who brought a broad experience not only of the Church but of the wider statutory and voluntary youth service.

Role of diocesan youth officers

8.10   A development of stronger links with local education authority youth services, other voluntary youth organisations and other denominational youth services has enhanced the quality of work with young people. Diocesan youth officers are often seen as a resource to other groups and agencies, particularly in the area of training and spirituality. They have been able to draw upon the gifts and skills of other professions for the benefit of the Church and its young people. As well as their supportive, advisory and training role diocesan youth officers have frequently identified and sought to fill gaps in provision for the Church's young people. Such opportunities have included camps, pilgrimages and other events for young people, training for youth leaders, international links and exchanges, and involvement with national events.

Diocesan youth officers have also played a significant part in supporting and developing local/parochial initiatives in youth work as well as offering larger events for young people and youth workers.

Initiatives by diocesan youth officers

8.11   In the mid 1980s the diocesan youth officer conference proposed an initiative for the provision of an introduction to youth work course for theological colleges. Syllabus guidelines were approved by the Board of Education, a consultation took place with the conference of theological college staff and this course was launched in January 1987. This short course gave an opportunity to:

●   reflect theologically about adolescence and working with young people

●   consider varieties of youth work practice and to identify good youth work practice

●   discover how to find and use appropriate resources available for work with young people.

The diocesan youth officer network encouraged debate and discussion about good practice. One initiative arising from this was negotiations with the Ecclesiastical Insurance Group to create a national youth and children's group insurance scheme in 1980.

The evolution of the Youth Fellowship

Anglican Youth

8.12   A significant organisation that contributed to the development of Youth Fellowships was the Anglican Young Peoples' Association (AYPA), which became very popular during the 1930s primarily in 'high' church parishes. Meetings of AYPA groups were planned to follow a regular structure based on its four main aims of 'worship, study, witness and service'. AYPA offered camps, national conferences and resource materials to help those running groups.

CPAS and CSSM

8.13   The growth of youth work in evangelical churches in the 1930s focused on a strategy to reach boys and girls from the upper middle classes who were 'largely out of touch with the Gospel'. Significant organisations adopting this approach were the Crusader Union and the Children's Special Service Mission (CSSM). In 1932 CSSM appointed Eric Nash to start a camping ministry amongst the top public schools in Britain. These camps were spread to include preparatory school boys and groups from less well-known public schools throughout the country. It is evident that large numbers of young people were to find faith through these camps and many young men involved were encouraged to seek ordination in the Anglican Church. In 1930 the Young Churchmen's Fellowship was set up, originally seeking to link together individual young adults in evangelical churches. By 1935 the Fellowship began to accept affiliation from numbers of young people in parish-based youth groups. Responding to the needs of these groups, the Young Churchmen's Fellowship began to supply a syllabus and list of recognised speakers who would be willing to visit the groups. The Young Churchmen's Fellowship was later to become part of the Church Pastoral Aid Society and change its name to the Church Youth Fellowship Association (CYFA). Another evangelical initiative started in the 1930s by Canon Herbert Taylor was called Pathfinders; it later joined with CPAS, specifically catering for 11- to 14-year-olds.

Other Youth Fellowships

8.14   During the 1960s a number of evangelical organisations founded in the US, started in England, notably Youth for Christ, Teen Challenge and Youth With A Mission.

Alongside the Youth Fellowship, aimed specifically at the Christian nurture of young people with the Church, many churches in the 1960s felt that they should offer an open youth club for young people from the local community. Whilst this pattern was widely followed by evangelical churches, it has been a difficult area of ministry to sustain and in the place of the open youth club evangelistic efforts tended to focus on major events using Christian rock bands or drama groups.

Residentials and festivals

8.15   It is important to recognise the crucial part that residential work, holidays and house parties have played in youth work over the years. Residential opportunities have served to encourage large numbers of young people in the faith and they have been a remarkable source of young leaders, not only in the field of youth work but also in the wider ministry of the Church.

The move towards larger Christian festivals as a means of reaching young people is evident in the existence of Greenbelt, which started in a Suffolk field in 1974, and Spring Harvest, which grew out of the Ministry of Music Gospel Outreach, as well as countless other events of this kind. For Christian young people this began to offer a sub-culture with its own language, pop music and festivals to attend. For Christian parents this was perhaps seen as a safe alternative to what was being offered by the secular world. For church leaders here was a whole way of expressing the faith which seemed to offer the chance of reaching out to young people outside the Church.

The Church of England Young People's Assembly

8.16   During the 1970s attempts were made in most sectors of the youth service to develop effective means of promoting the participation of young people. The General Synod Board of Education promoted the creation of the Church of England Young People's Assembly (CEYPA) with the following underlying aims:

- to provide a visible national forum within the Church of England for the expression of young adult opinion

- to encourage the nomination of young adults as candidates in elections to General Synod

- to develop effective means to promote young adult participation in Church and society

- to model good practice in all of these aims.

Significant progress was made towards the achievement of these aims, notably:

- an annual national conference of young adults

- supportive work in the recruitment and preparation of candidates for nomination in General Synod elections

- a number of dioceses initiated their own youth assemblies or conferences.

However, a number of drawbacks hampered these aims. Firstly, the attempt to operate this entirely by the voluntary efforts of a nationwide group of young adults was ambitious and less than effective. Secondly, it was unclear whether the conference was open to all those 'affiliated' to CEYPA or open to all, and this confusion resulted in loss of confidence in some dioceses.

Aims of CEYPA *from* 1988 *onwards*

8.17   In 1988 a consultation day to assess current and future needs in promoting young adult involvement in the Church of England included members of the last standing committee of CEYPA, representatives of youth work organisations in the Church of England, diocesan youth officers and National Youth Office staff. The prime needs to be met by any national provision was seen as being:

- to recognise that participation implies the inter-dependence of young people and adults

- to provide a national focal point by means of which the contribution of young people to the life and ministry of the Church may be recognised and affirmed

- to **avoid** the creation of a Youth Synod

- to ensure that young people receive information about every opportunity and means of involvement at local and national level

- to ensure consistency and continuity in whatever provision is made.

Following this consultation, and bearing in mind the resolution from the Lambeth Conference in 1988 encouraging youth involvement in the life of the dioceses and the provinces at every level, the following recommendations were made:

- that there should be an annual youth forum bringing together at national level a widely representative group of young people in order to:

- provide a focus for young people's involvement in the mission and ministry of the Church

- affirm that young people need to be heard

- enable the development of competence among some young people to encourage their further participation

- provide a stimulus to promote involvement of young people in parishes and dioceses

- that there should be a major conference for young people every three years.

8.18   The National Young Adult Forum initiative led to several dioceses creating similar bodies offering a process by which young adults could contribute to and be involved in the decision-making processes of the Church. An initiative in the early 1990s to invite a young adult observer group to General Synod meetings in York proved to be a beneficial experience for both the young people involved and members of General Synod. The Young Adult Network which started as a result of this initiative was concerned to support young people who had been elected as representatives onto parochial church councils and deanery synods.

General Synod Youth Affairs Group

8.19   Drawing together representatives from Anglican youth work agencies including the diocesan youth officer network, the General Synod Youth Affairs Group proved to be a valuable forum for sharing ideas and taking initiatives. It was able to address the following:

- the implications of the Educational Reform Bill for youth work in the Church of England

- the variety of models of young adult participation

- the monitoring of headquarter's grants for national voluntary youth organisations and the introduction of programme funding through the Department for Education

- initiatives following on from 'Faith in the City' and 'Faith in the Countryside'

- the support of full-time youth workers in the Church of England

- the proposal for a Youth Sunday within the Church calendar

- vocational work with young people.

Future trends

8.20   There are many influences on youth work and it is very difficult to forecast how it will develop in the future. However three particular strands converging on youth work today will strongly affect practice into the next century. The first is the present and future financing and prioritising of youth work and education by local authorities, government and voluntary agencies. The second is the dramatic change in young people's education with the huge majority now going on to further education, which is either academic or vocational. The third is the fragmenting of culture and value (post-modernism) which challenges any institution where a single set orthodoxy and expected way of behaving is a major part of that institution.

Financing and Prioritising youth work

8.21   In the last decade constant pressure has been placed on local authorities to decrease their spending on community services. Youth services have not escaped these pressures and many have been called to make severe reductions to the facilities and services available to young people. Corresponding pressure has been felt by schools and with decreased budgets the core elements of the curriculum are protected at the expense of informal education so they are less able to respond to social as opposed to educational needs.

Other sites for youth work include further education colleges which have recently experienced rapid growth. This growth has been at a time of limited funding and in a climate of individual choice so youth work has been seen as a way of helping the person to engage with their formal education rather than to significantly extend the curriculum in terms of community and social development. Some colleges do employ youth workers but these are more likely to be youth counsellors geared to solving individual problems rather than community-based youth workers.

In the present climate this pattern of restricted funding is likely to continue and will have an enormous effect on the shape of the youth service.

Changes in patterns of education

8.22   Recent development in patterns of education mean that for the first time in our history most young people are spending the formative years of 16 to 19 in educational institutions. The numbers of young people leaving education at 16 years has reduced dramatically and a majority (recently estimated as between 80 and 90 per cent) will stay on at college pursuing either vocational or academic qualifications. Vocational qualifications on offer at further education colleges are perceived as the new route into skilled and semi-skilled jobs. Would- be hairdressers, plumbers, secretaries and electricians will move from school into further education and then possibly into higher education before they start earning in the workplace.

The increase in numbers of young people entering the further and higher education colleges has to be acknowledged and recognised not only in terms of youth work but also on the impact for the community.

Changes in how institutions operate

8.23   There have been enormous changes in how institutions operate since the origins of the youth service. These have had an impact on youth work both inside the Church and in society. In a post-modernist world, institutions have to operate within a culture of many meanings and one where the individual is encouraged to 'customise' his or her life. Young people in the late twentieth century expect to have a whole range of options from which they can design education, leisure time, their wardrobe or their music. Life is like a department store where the merchandise is on offer and is 'sold hard' and the individual wanders and models his/her life according to individual preferences (see paragraphs 1.8-11).

Consequences of current change

8.24   These shifts in culture and occupation are dramatic and will have a huge effect on the shape of youth work for the next century. The role of local authorities and the strictures on spending will dictate the investment in this work.

If youth work has a continuing future, there has to be strategic thinking and planning. As it is impossible to predict exactly what will be the key influences some possible strands are explored below.

Patterns of youth work

8.25   Many of the existing patterns of youth work which focus on particular issues, activities, or interests are likely to continue. However, the growing pressures on young people to devote increasing amounts of time to their educational work may mean that they will be less able to make substantial and regular commitments to one group or club. Thus opportunities for informal social education could be greatly diminished. Consultation with young people to find out what they want and to engage with them to work toward this is crucial to find new patterns of youth work which will help their social education as well as enable them to pursue their own interests.

Work within schools and colleges

8.26   As most of the young people are within educational institutions these are the obvious points of contact. Chaplains provide a particular service, but local churches can do much more to work with local educational institutions. Either at parish or diocesan levels the Church can work with the schools and colleges to identify what kind of provision young people want and need as they study; the Church can then put in resources and support for this work.

Keying into other thinking in the Church

8.27   It is vitally important that work with and by young people is able to inform consultations regarding the future of ministry. Within the Church there is a move towards the development of local and collaborative ministry. A recent national consultation sponsored by the Edward King Institute drew thirty dioceses. Similarly the structures of the Church have been examined by the Turnbull Commission who have proposed changes. It is important that work with and by young people is part of these deliberations and that youth work is integral to future trends in ministry.

Keying into other thinking in the society

8.28   The Church has a significant contribution to make in the wider society. Where youth work cuts have disadvantaged young people in the community, it is important that those in the Church, find ways of challenging any such reduction in service. The partnerships that those in the Church have with colleagues in local authorities is crucial both to challenge cutbacks and, if these challenges fail to work, to limit the damage of these cuts.

Conclusion

8.29   The Church of England, both as an institution and through its individual members, has played a vital part in the formation and sustaining of the youth service in England. It is important that there is an awareness of the pioneering contribution of the Church and other Christians and Christian organisations to youth work and that this spirit is continued today.

If the Church is to be part of the continuing debate, there must be strategic thinking about the work with young people at every level of the Church. Old methods of youth work need to be examined and considered and serious consultation undertaken with young people. The resources to do this must be a central priority of the Church.

9

Recommendations and Objectives

9.1   As the research for this report was being compiled, it became apparent that a vision for the Church was emerging – a vision shared from north to south and from east to west of the country. In the nationwide consultations the report was endorsed, welcomed and affirmed by young people and those who work with young people.

The vision is for a Church which takes young people seriously. It is a Church where young people fully and actively participate at every level. It is a Church which is built on good relationships, where young people particularly are concerned, not only with each other, but with those inside and outside the Church. It is a Church where there is a good theological understanding of why and how it goes about its work with young people. It is a Church which recognises that work of this quality needs resources and has the faith and courage to commit significant resources to the young people in the Church.

9.2   This report covers the whole scope of the Church's work with young people. As well as the areas highlighted above, listed below are sixteen visions for the Church. Following these there are the Working Party's recommendations of ways in which these visions can become a reality.

In the second part of the chapter, these same issues have been addressed through the nationwide consultations by young people, youth workers and others working in the Church with young people. They have produced some very specific objectives based on their 'grass root' knowledge which are ideas that individuals, parishes, deaneries, dioceses and communities can set themselves to help bring the vision of the Church described above closer.

9.3   This report is not to be read once and put down, it is to be used. It covers a huge range and area of the Church's work with young people. It is not expected that all areas are attempted at once.

It is very important that the range and diversity of the visions and recommendations do not discourage the already hard-pressed youth worker/clergy/parent or young person. Much excellent work already goes on and one of the aims of the report is to acknowledge and build on this.

The recommendations and the ideas from the consultation are to be used with the experience of the reader and others in the community to help to improve the existing work.

9.4   The report will span the millenium. It is not intended to be implemented in full immediately; rather, it is hoped that people will work with it, setting one or two specific objectives, meet these and move on to one or two more, so that there is a progressive and upward movement to achieve the vision.

Recommendations from the Working Party

1.   We have a vision of a Church which takes young people and youth work seriously (see paragraph 4.29).

1.1   *We assert that the allocation of resources is paramount to taking this work seriously. One third of the population is under twenty-five; with this in mind we recommend that the Church examines its budgets and other resources at every level and reallocates these to reflect the distribution in population (see paragraphs 6.31-35).*

1.2   *We recommend that each diocese, deanery and parish agrees what its commitment is for work with young people, carries out an audit of resources allocated to youth work, and plans and implements changes in line with its commitment.*

1.3   *We recommend that consultations on all aspects of youth work and the Church should be set up with young people to decide future plans and priorities (see paragraphs 4.21-25).*

1.4   *We recommend that the chapter on theology in this report is debated and discussed at all levels in the Church (see chapter 2).*

2.   We have a vision of a Church which is committed to outreach and mission amongst and by young people and values young people as they share their faith (see paragraph 5.15).

2.1   *We recommend that outreach work is made a significant priority at all levels of the Church. We recommend that models of outreach are established or existing work specifically identified which could act as inspirational examples or training placements.*

2.2   *We recommend that the Church at every level should find ways to ensure that the role of young people in sharing their faith and being involved in mission is valued, recognised, supported and affirmed.*

2.3   We recognise the enormous benefit that young people gain from having opportunities to take part in special events, groups, retreats and outreach missions. We recommend that these are supported by the Church at every level (see paragraphs 3.18-26).

2.4   We recommend that opportunities are created for young people to explore ideas of mission and outreach ecumenically with other denominations (see paragraph 7.25).

3.   We have a vision of a Church where young people are leaders and innovators (see paragraph 4.27).

3.1   We recommend that young people are offered training in leadership (see paragraphs 6.27 and 5.4).

3.2   We recommend that networks are formed which can be used for training and provide a framework of mutual accountability, support and encouragement (see chapter 6).

3.3   We recommend that young people's roles in planning and delivering youth work and other work for the Church and the community is valued, supported, endorsed and resourced.

3.4   We recommend that young people are enabled to play full and active roles in the development and practice of collaborative ministry in their local church (see paragraphs 8.27).

4.   We have a vision of a Church in which young people are consulted and participate in decision making at all levels in the Church so that they have involvement as full members of the Body of Christ (see paragraphs 4.22-8).

4.1   We recommend that the Church examines structures and procedures at every level of decision-making to check that these do not inhibit young people's representation and participation.

4.2   We recommend that at each level of decision-making young people should be present, and each diocese, deanery or PCC should agree a plan on how this is achieved (for example quotas).

4.3   We recommend that consultation events (for example a Youth Forum) are arranged with young people. This is in addition to young people being encouraged to participate in other Church structures (see paragraph 4.22).

4.4   We recommend that young people are offered training and support (for example mentors) to help them to better participate in the structures of the Church.

4.5   We recommend that all members of PCCs, deanery synods, diocesan synods and General Synod should have access to training to help them to communicate with and get the most from young people's participation.

5.   We have a vision of a Church which values young people's spirituality. (see chapter 3).

5.1   We recommend that opportunities are made where the faith and experience of young people is nurtured and shared with other Christians in a spirit of mutual respect and learning.

5.2   We recognise that young people are 'called' both to secular occupations and to work within the Church and recommend that the Church investigates and implements ways for them to explore their calling (see paragraph 3.35).

5.3   We recognise the value of older Christians, parents and grandparents in the faith development of young people and recommend that those in the Church are encouraged to find ways of valuing and enhancing these relationships (see paragraphs 5.11-14).

6.   We have a vision of a Church where young people plan, lead and take part in worship, and help develop new ways to worship (see paragraphs 4.2-10).

6.1   We recommend that a bank of resource material and ideas relating to new ways of worship be kept at diocesan and national level and that opportunities are made to share these. We also encourage the formation of worship study centres to act as a focus of worship ideas and to provide training.

6.2   We recommend that the lessons learnt from early work with Local Ecumenical Projects' approach to Canon Law are used when considering local liturgical experimentation with young people (see paragraph 4.11).

6.3   We recommend that diocesan advisory groups be set up to work with 'alternative' or new worship initiatives to offer them a framework of support and accountability (see paragraphs 4.13-17).

6.4   We recommend that liturgical revision groups should consult with young people and use their input and perspectives.

7.   We have a vision of a Church that understands, learns from, and supports young people as they work with issues such as the environment, homelessness, unemployment, family breakdown and depression (see paragraph 1.4).

7.1   We recommend that opportunities are made through special projects and in parish life for young people to share with others by giving and receiving support (see paragraph 1.23-30).

7.2   We recommend training for youth workers, clergy and others working with young people which is sensitive to these issues (see paragraph 6.45).

7.3   We recognise the sensitivity and commitment many young people have to issues of justice, peace and the environment and recommend that ways are found to incorporate young people's concerns into the mission and work of the Church (see paragraph 1.7).

7.4   We recommend that people who take youth work seriously must also take seriously matters of human sexuality.

7.5   We recommend that links between Church youth workers and those of other faiths be adequately resourced, especially in multi-racial areas (see paragraph 1.6).

8.   We have a vision of a Church which supports and is open to all young people including those who are marginalised and discriminated against (see paragraphs 1.4-7).

8.1   We recognise the many young people who are marginalised and discriminated against. We recommend that the Church identifies marginalised groups and works with them towards equality, both in the Church and in society.

8.2   We recognise tensions in some multi-cultural/racial communities and recommend improved communications and joint working with other groups for better understanding amongst young people and the wider community (see paragraph 1.6).

8.3   We recommend that projects and clubs should have an equal opportunity policy and regular equal opportunity audits (see paragraphs 6.41-42).

9.   We have a vision of a Church where youth work is built upon good relationships with young people (see paragraphs 5.1-14).

9.1   We recognise that relationships are at the heart of youth work and that this involves listening to young people, loving them and sharing the gospel and should involve all members of the Church (see paragraph 5.19).

9.2   We recommend that young people are informed, consulted and valued both individually and within the structures of the Church.

9.3   We recommend that outreach work starts with young people 'where they are' in a spirit of clarity and openness, and that the Christian ethic of honesty, trust and caring is central to this work (see paragraph 5.16).

10. We have a vision of a Church where there is 'good practice' in all of its work with young people and the role of diocesan youth officers in maintaining and supporting this work is recognised (see chapter 6 and paragraphs 8.8-11).

10.1 *We recommend that the role of the diocesan youth officers and their networks is acknowledged by parishes, dioceses and nationally, and real commitment made to increasing the range and effectiveness of their work (see paragraphs 7.2-6 and 7.27).*

10.2 *We recommend that training and support is available for all youth workers so that their work is of the highest quality and reflects good practice throughout (see paragraphs 6.7-32).*

10.3 *We recommend that all parishes ensure that all youth workers, whether paid or unpaid, are clear about the scope and the responsibilities of their work and know to whom they are responsible and accountable (see paragraphs 6.8 and 6.16-23).*

10.4 *We recommend that all parishes, deaneries and dioceses, acquaint themselves with their legal responsibilities concerning young people and regulate their youth work in accordance with these, e.g.* Safe from Harm *and the* Children Act, *minibus requirements, etc. (see paragraphs 6.40-46).*

11. We have a vision of a Church in which those who work with young people are of a high calibre, and are valued and affirmed by the Church and offered a framework of training, accountability and support (see chapter 6).

11.1 *We recommend that all youth workers are supported both spiritually and in their youth work practice (see paragraph 6.11-12).*

11.2 *We recommend that all parishes should ensure their youth workers have a clear job description and have access to training, have a professional youth work supervisor, and a line manager to help manage practice (see paragraph 6.20-23).*

11.3 *We recommend that every youth worker has a support group which meets his or her spiritual needs and prays regularly for the work. We also recommend that the work is regularly prayed for by the wider Church (see paragraph 6.20-21).*

11.4 *We recommend that youth work is formally recognised and affirmed by the Church and that the General Synod Board of Education in consultation with the General Synod Board of Mission be charged to investigate and implement this. We bring to their notice the example of the Lutheran Church where youth workers are part of the diaconate (see paragraph 6.31).*

11.5   We recommend the development of training for full-time Christian youth workers which combines the Professional National Youth Agency Accreditation with a theological education.

11.6   We recommend that resources be found for a support network for full-time youth workers in churches and Christian projects. We recommend that diocesan guidelines be available on conditions of service, specified training and lines of responsibility to ensure this work is of the best quality. We also recommend that these workers should be part of a diocesan network (see paragraph 6.39-42).

11.7   We recognise that the calling of many Christians is to work in secular situations with young people and recommend that dioceses reflect on this and find ways to support and encourage these people (see paragraph 6.3).

12.   We have a vision of a Church where clergy training has a significant emphasis on work with young people (see paragraph 6.3 + 6.44-5).

12.1   We recommend that theological colleges should provide youth work modules to improve the understanding and youth work skills of all clergy.

12.2   We recognise that some people are called both to youth work and to be clergy. We recommend that the opportunity to specialise in youth work as part of a ministry should be explored.

12.3   We recommend and affirm the use of the diocesan youth officer network as a resource for either initial, or post-ordination training.

13.   We have a vision of a Church which encourages partnerships with other organisations which work with young people (see chapter 7).

13.1   We recognise the crucial work which is being done by schools, colleges and universities and recommend that all existing partnership work is endorsed, resourced and encouraged and that joint work should be part of future plans (see paragraphs 3.27-33).

13.2   We recognise the decrease in youth work funding in other agencies and recommend joint work and partnership as a way to share resources, for example, premises, staff, projects, policy-making and training and to promote together the proper financing of youth work (see chapter 7).

13.3   We recognise the importance of employing full-time workers and officers to establish and maintain links with full-time local authority colleagues and colleagues in voluntary organisations, and recommend that these posts are maintained or created at all levels of the Church (see paragraphs 7.7-12).

13.4   We recommend that the Church at diocesan, deanery and parish levels should actively seek an ongoing dialogue with their local authority about the contribution that the Church could make to the youth service in the area.

13.5　We recommend that the Church, especially at local level, should be made aware of and encouraged to take up both a) the range of aid and support available to it from the local authority; and b) the range of opportunities for the young people in its youth groups to participate in events and activities with young people from other groups and clubs (see paragraphs 7.7-12).

13.6　We recommend that the Church at all levels considers and keeps under regular review how the potential of partnership with the uniformed organisations can be more effectively realised (see paragraphs 7.13-20).

14.　We have a vision of a Church which encourages partnerships with other denominations and Christian organisations which work with young people (see chapter 7).

14.1　We recommend that links between young people and youth workers of different denominations is well resourced and a vision for this work is developed at all levels of the Church (see paragraph 7.25).

14.2　We value and appreciate Christian organisations which work with young people and recommend that the full potential of these partnerships should be explored and worked towards (see paragraph 7.21-24).

15.　We have a vision of a Church which sees youth work as one part of a faith journey which continues and develops as young people become older and their life circumstances change (see chapter 3).

15.1　We recognise that youth work happens at one stage in a person's faith journey and relationship with the Church. We recommend that ways are explored to continue and sustain this journey and relationship into adult life (see paragraphs 3.1-12).

15.2　We recommend that there is a follow-up of confirmation candidates, to encourage a continuing relationship with the Church (see paragraphs 5.34-39).

15.3　We recognise that there are opportunities to build relationships with young people as they marry in Church or bring their children for baptism or dedication. We recommend that this area of the Churchs' work is explored and ways are found to share good practice (see paragraphs 5.30-32).

16.　We have a vision of a Church which appreciates that young people have their own ways of expressing themselves and distinct cultures which they will bring to the Church (see chapter 1).

16.1　We recommend that the distinct cultures of young people are acknowledged, encouraged and integrated into Church structures and the thinking of the Church (see paragraphs 1.8-12).

16.2   *We recommend that specific occasions for young people to explore their worship and mission in the light of their own experience are arranged at all levels of the Church (see paragraphs 3.14 and 4.4).*

Specific objectives set by the consultations

9.5   The report was written on the results of extensive research and survey throughout England. When the report was in its first draft it was taken to all six regions of the country to check out whether the issues identified through the research corresponded to the issues that young people and youth workers were dealing with in their own parishes and situations.

As a result of these consultations not only were there additions and corrections to the central text but the local groups provided specific ways that the vision of the report can be realised in their own working settings.

One of the points that was fed back from all of the consultations was that those involved would have liked to have worked for a longer time to set specific objectives which were more comprehensive.

What we have in these specific objectives is not a complete set of aims and suggested courses of action. The list does provide a range of starting-points based on many years of experience and reflection, which will help those reading the report to try new things to improve youth work.

We suggest that if your parish, deanery, or diocese is serious about improving its work with young people, then some of these objectives should be used as a starting-point to effect real change.

Key to Consultations

North West Region:	+Ke	Kendal	+SH	Stockton Heath
North East Region:	+Ta	Tadcaster	+Du	Durham
Midlands Region:	+Nt	Nottingham		
Eastern Region:	+KL	King's Lynn	+SW	Saffron Walden
South West Region:	+St	Street	+Tr	Truro
South East Region:	+Gu	Guildford		

1. We have a vision of a Church which takes young people and youth work seriously (see paragraph 4.29).

Objectives from Consultations

General

1. Recognise the young people who are already part of the Church and use their strengths and achievements. +Tr +Ke

2. Make sure there are appropriate resources in deaneries, dioceses and nationally for youth work. +Ke +SH

3. Ensure clergy and lay people are trained in youth work. +Tr

4. Provide a challenging programme of activities and opportunities for young people at all levels of the Church. +Ke

5. Support peer interchange, i.e. outside church circle. +Ke

6. Make *Youth A Part* available to the young people. +Gu

Parish

1. Include youth work in the annual parish budget and ensure there are good resources available. +Tr +Du +Ke

2. Give young people responsibilities (e.g. sidesperson, readers . . .). +Tr

3. Make a 'youth ghetto' in the Church where young people control access to the space. +St

4. PCC and young people to take part in an exercise to examine values (e.g. Bridge Building exercise in Spectrum 2). +St

5. Include youth work in the PCC agenda regularly, not as Any Other Business. +Du +Gu +SH

6. Adopt a parish policy for youth work, including: Mission Statement, Objectives and Guidelines. +Du +SH

7. Encourage and offer support and back up to young people who wish to be on PCC or synod. +St +Gu +Ke

8. Ensure that young people who are consulted or are members of the PCC are not just chosen or proposed by the incumbent (to give a wider representation). +Gu

9. Form a young people's committee with specific range of responsibilities. +Ke

10. Invite young people to sub-committees of PCC and deanery meetings to give their views. +Du +Gu

11. Use young people to survey Church members over various issues (and develop young people's views in the process). +Du

12. Employ or appoint youth workers at parish or deanery level. +Du

13. Give a personal invitation to young people to participate in an event/activity/committee. +SH

Deanery
1. Set up a support network for young people within a deanery or college catchment area which would offer personal support and counselling. +St +Ke

2. Appoint deanery youth link person to share information, assist events, activities, service youth forum, etc. +Du

Diocese
1. Make resources available for pro-active support at diocesan level. +Ke

2. Invite young people to a diocesan synod, or hold a young people's synod. +Gu

2. We have a vision of a Church which is committed to outreach and mission amongst and by young people and values young people as they share their faith (see paragraph 5.15)

Objectives from Consultations

General
1. Churches (of different denominations) to find ways of working together at all levels for the benefit of young people rather than for the denomination.

2. Allow enough time for youth opportunities to work. Think long term. +Ke

3. Arrange good consultations between youth workers and young people at all levels. +SW

4. Create opportunities for young people to take leadership roles and encourage them to try new things. +SW

5. Recognise the importance in relationships in outreach initiatives, and to encourage and support these.

Parish

1. Work out a mission statement and how to implement it. +Ta

2. Explore, select and use relevant models, real and radical, to engage with the local community and be really effective. +Ta

3. Identify organisations active in missions and plan ways of working together. +Ta

4. Value young people's experience continually. +Ta

5. Ensure through training and supervision that there is a good under-standing of the responsibility of youth workers for the young people and vice versa. +SW

6. Plan events with young people which are fun. These can be all-age events as well as specifically for young people. +Ke

7. Recognise the commitments young people have outside Church and arrange flexible programmes without too much pressure. +Ke

Deanery

1. Encourage deaneries, especially in rural areas, to work collabora-tively to increase resources and opportunities. +Ta

2. Value deanery boundaries, but also use natural networks and clus-ters of churches for joint working. +Ta

Diocese

1. Identify Christian partnerships who are active in mission, plan to work together. +Ta

2. Extend the resourcing role of the diocese to enable work in the network. +Ta

National

1. Understand what is meant by 'mission'. +Ta

2. Commitment to the vision of a young Church, in theory and by locating resources and planning how this should happen. +Ta

3. We have a vision of a Church where young people are leaders, innovators (see paragraph 4.27).

General

1. Allow enough time for youth opportunities to work. Think long term. +Ke

2.   Arrange good consultations between youth workers and young people at all levels. +SW

3.   Ensure through training and supervision that there is a good understanding of the responsibility of youth workers for the young people and vice versa. +SW

3.   Create opportunities for young people to take leadership roles and encourage them to try new things. +SW

Parish
1.   Value young people's experience continually. +Ta

2.   Ensure proper representation on PCCs. +Ta +SW

3.   Plan events with young people which are fun. These can be all-age events as well as specifically for young people. +Ke

4.   Recognise the commitments young people have outside church and arrange flexible programmes without too much pressure. +Ke

Deanery
1.   Make a commitment to support young people in the structures. Plan how this commitment is exercised. +Ta

Diocese
1.   Make space in diocesan newsletters/magazines for young people's articles. +Ta

2.   Offer resources, videos/teaching/examples on how to involve young people. +Ta

3.   Ensure young people are able to stand on synod. +Ta

4.   Give official recognition to those working with young people. +Ta +SH

National
1.   Commitment to the vision of a young Church, in theory and by locating resources and planning how this should happen. +Ta

Other
1.   Check with other agencies, including the uniformed organisations, how they involve and include young people, arrange joint consultation/training. +Ta +Ke

2.   Recognise the power difference between young people and adults and ensure that young people are being listened to, treated as equals, given time and have their contributions valued and used. +Ke +SW

4.   We have a vision of a Church in which young people are consulted and participate in decision making at all levels in the Church so that they have involvement as full members of the Body of Christ (see paragraphs 4.22-28).

Objectives from Consultations

General
1.   Train and support adults to listen and respond to young people positively. +Ta

2.   Give young people access to participation in decision making structures of the Church at all levels. +SH +Gu

3.   Reduce the age limit for PCC membership and deanery synod. +Gu

Parish
1.   Ensure that young people are represented, be part of or report to the PCC, worship, service committees. +Ta

2.   Include young people (elected or co-opted) on PCCs. +Gu

3.   Make a survey of young people's work which shows funding and resources. +Ta

4.   Check the representation of young people on committees and in decision-making groups within the Church. +Ta

5.   Hold a consultation meeting with young people. Find an 'unbiased' person to ask what they are thinking about worship, parish matters, youth work, etc. Encourage them to talk freely. +Ta

6.   Allow young people to choose their youth workers. +Ta

Deanery
1.   Get representatives from all parishes for a youth synod. +Ta

2.   Empower young people to set the agenda for a synod. +Ta

3.   Include young people (elected or co-opted) on deanery synod. +Gu

4.   Have a 'youth work coordinator' in each deanery. +Gu

Diocesan

1.   Youth representatives to synod (supported and trained). +Ta +Gu

2.   Youth representatives to Bishop's Council. +Ta

National

1.   Appoint a bishop with a special concern for youth work and to represent the interests of young people at General Synod and other meetings. +Gu

5.   We have a vision of a Church which values young people's spirituality (see chapter 3).

Objectives from Consultations

General

1.   Have a concept of spirituality which is constantly developing and growing. +Nt

2.   Value 'older' Christians in faith development and find ways to encourage a spirit of mutual respect and learning between older and younger people.

3.   Value peers, other Church members and parents.

4.   Share ecumenically and with those of other faiths.

Parish

1.   Recognise (formally and informally) the role of older Christians and find ways for older people to partner or sponsor young people so that the responsibility to work with young people as they develop their faith is seen as belonging to them as well as to the priest. +Ke +Nt

2.   Encourage older people to act as advocates for young people, ensure that they are aware of what young people are thinking and make their case at PCCs, etc. +Ke

3.   Use the model of joining young and older members with the whole congregation to get an integration of these ideas of cross-communication and support. +Ke

4.   Keep the services inclusive – explain parts of the Church, the calendar, service, etc. and keep an eye on language. +Ke

5.   Create an opportunity to exchange with other youth groups to share faith and visions, frustrations and food. +Ke

6.   Invite 'older members' to come to youth groups. +Nt

7.   Accept existing young people in the congregation as people in their own right, not as Mr Smith's son or daughter. +Nt

8.   Be open to people coming back from a residential, retreat, or time away. Be aware that they may have experienced spiritual challenge and growth and find ways for people to voice and share this in the parish. +Nt

Deanery

1.   Arrange meetings of young people in other parishes or ecumenically with a focus on spiritual growth and exploration. +Nt

2.   Find ways to encourage parishes to work together to serve all young people in the deanery, rather than seeing their churches as separate entities. +Nt

Diocese

1.   Arrange opportunities for young people to reflect, participate in celebration, and nurture their faith. +Nt

6.   We have a vision of a Church where young people plan, lead and take part in worship, and help develop new ways to worship (see paragraphs 4.2-10).

Objectives from Consultations

General

1.   Encourage and arrange use of computer internet for young people to comment on different forms of worship. +Ke

2.   Work in partnership with other denominations to share worship ideas and services. +Gu

3.   Ensure there is consultation with young people at all levels.

Parish

1.   Ensure that young people are aware of their responsibility and encourage young people to make a range of different contributions to a wide variety of services (not just family service and Youth Sunday). +Gu +Ke

2.   Include young people in 'all age' worship teams to plan services. +SW

3.   Set up smaller worship services led by young people, possibly on days other than Sunday. +Gu +SW

4.   Value young people and be aware of their worship needs and preferences. Arrange consultations to find out what these preferences are. +Ke

5.   Have regular 'official' services led by young people, e.g. Youth Sunday +SW

6.   Educate older people so that they know that youth services do not necessarily have to be loud or 'alternative'. +SW

7.   Avoid making other Church members uncomfortable. +Du

Deanery

1.   Share resources about fresh ideas for 'experimental worship' and youth services. +SW

2.   Invite young people from clusters of churches to share worship, especially in rural areas where young people may be isolated. +Ke

Diocese

1.   Arrange large-scale worship and celebration events for young people. Make sure these are well publicised. +Ke +SW +Gu +Du

2.   Arrange training/workshop events to share ideas about worship, liturgy and alternative music (using a range of instruments, including combs). +Ke

National

1.   Promote radio and television youth led worship. +Gu

2.   Publish a youth magazine where ideas about worship, etc can be shared. +Gu

3.   Work with funding agencies to locate resources for worship. +Gu

4.   Set up a worship study centre to offer a focus for worship ideas and provide training.

7.   We have a vision of a Church which understands, learns from, and supports young people as they work with issues such as the environment, homelessness, unemployment, family breakdown and depression (see paragraph 1.4).

Objectives from Consultations

Parish

1. Find out who in the congregation has listening/counselling skills. +SW +Tr

2. Co-ordinate skills and use training to build up a team. Advertise this team. Use notice boards, announce in church, parish magazine. +SW

3. All members to talk with young people about matters that concern them, don't wait to be asked. +SW

4. Ensure that there is trust and that people can be confident in the relationships (confidentiality). Make time and space to work through problems with young people. +Tr +SW

5. Find out what other agencies can help young people and build up a parish resource. Use those both in and outside the Church with specialist knowledge. +SW +Tr

6. Arrange a focus group or help line, encourage a general awareness and sensitivity to pick up any problems. +Tr

7. Air issues that are not generally talked about in special services, find other ways to become aware of issues which young people manage. +SW +Tr

8. Organise youth group meetings and discussions. +SW

9. Find ways that youth groups can present issues to the Church or the local media, make sure support is available for this. +SW

10. Organise a young people's forum/Junior PCC to debate certain issues and decide on actions. +Tr

11. Extend invitations to local schools to discuss, explore issues, or go into schools. +SW

12. Use youth workers as 'go-betweens' or advocates. +SW

Diocese

1. Make sure that there is training available for the youth workers. +SW

2. Build up a diocesan resource of special knowledge and ideas. +SW

8.   We have a vision of a Church which supports and is open to all young people including those who are marginalised and discriminated against (see paragraphs 1.4-7).

Objectives from Consultations

General
1. Realise that the Church has much to learn from those it marginalises. +Nt

Parish
1. Encourage the congregation to realise that everyone is responsible for welcoming people into the parish and that this welcome is especially important for those who are perceived to be 'different'. +Nt

2. Draw up an equal opportunities policy for your parish, make sure that it is continually assessed, evaluated and developed. +Nt

3. Acknowledge the way that individuals in the community are experiencing pain, prejudice and alienation and find ways as a community to challenge and attend to this. Realise that the process between the individual and the community is two way. +Nt

4. Take risks within the community to challenge and work to make the Church and the society less prejudiced. +Nt

9. **We have a vision of a Church where youth work is built upon good relationships with young people** (see paragraphs 5.1-14).

Objectives from Consultations

Parish
1. Involve young people in outreach both to other young people and to other age groups. +SH

2. Be prepared to take risks, while having responsibility for tasks given. +SH

3. Meet young people on their territory initially, so that they may feel confident and secure. +Tr +SW

4. Work with young people at the things that they want to do at first and then introduce other things, e.g. faith, spirituality, etc. +Tr +SW +SH

5. Encourage relationships between young people, through group activities, residentials, etc. Then work to strengthen the relationships between these groups and older people. +Tr +SH

6. Be sensitive to the age of young people and the activity. Some can be 'all-age'; others have to have a tighter age band. +Tr

7.   Encourage tolerance. +Tr

8.   Consult with the young people as to how to improve communications, etc. +Tr

9.   Run all-age activities and make sure young people have responsibility at these times. +SW

10. Build up trust in relationships by ensuring that there is honesty, respect and commitment. Use training to identify and work on these points. +SW +SH

11. Invite PCC to attend a youth meeting. +SW +St

12. Run open youth clubs in the Church to encourage 'non-Church' people to attend. +SH

13. Let young people know that they are part of the Church family and are welcome. +SH

14. Work with the homeless and unemployed either from the Church or through supporting projects. +SH

15. Use older people or youth workers to bridge the gap between young people and the structures of the Church. +SH

16. Build up contact with schools, get to know Christian staff and build relationships between the Church and the school. +Tr

17. Encourage young people to invite older members of the congregation and the clergy to youth group or for a meal. +St

Diocese

1.   Run training events which focus on building relationships for youth workers and others. +SW +SH

10.   We have a vision of a Church where there is 'good practice' in all of its work with young people and the role of diocesan youth officers in maintaining and supporting this work is recognised (see chapter 6 and paragraphs 8.8-11).

Objectives from Consultations

General

1.   Officially recognise youth workers and youth work and make youth work a valid ministry within the church. +KL

2. Recognise that training (both initial and ongoing) is essential in maintaining good practice. Ensure that this is available for all youth workers, paid and unpaid. +Tr

3. Introduce issues of good practice sensitively so that it does not 'frighten off' volunteers. +Tr

Parish
1. Parishes to ensure that their youth work is safe and follows good practice guidelines. +Tr

Diocese
1. Ensure that each diocese has at least one full time Diocesan Youth Officer with adequate office support and resources. +KL +Tr

2. Arrange and encourage links between DYO team, clergy and youth workers. Make sure that churches that employ youth workers inform the diocese and work with the Diocesan Youth Officer, to gain access to support, resources and training. +Tr

3. Employ parish liaison officers to keep good communication between the dioceses and the parishes. +Tr

National
1. Offer validation and formal recognition of youth workers, with national criteria and expectations. +Tr

2. Arrange an annual conference of youth workers in the Church. +Tr

3. Establish and promote national standards regarding use of consent forms, vetting of leaders, checking buildings, etc. +Tr

11. We have a vision of a Church in which those who work with young people are of a high calibre, and are valued and affirmed by the Church and offered a framework of training, accountability and support (see chapter 6).

Objectives from Consultations

General
1. Present the report to every congregation (in the main service) in England. +KL

2. Recognise that being ordained is not an automatic qualification for youth work and clergy should receive training in this. +Gu

3. Budget for youth work adequately at all levels of Church work. +Nt

Parish

1. Affirm youth workers in the parish, e.g. by clergy within ordinary services. Offer proper recognition by the parish that this is a special task and commission them to it. +Nt +Gu

2. Allocate proper finance and resources through the PCC for youth work and make sure that those doing the work have access to these resources. +Nt +Gu

3. Recognise good role models within the older generation. +KL

4. Support for youth workers – prayer and practical. Vicars should meet with their youth workers on a regular basis. +Nt +Gu

5. Adopt the youth leader as an ex-officio member of the PCC. +Gu

6. Arrange for clergy to be present at youth leaders meetings. +Nt

7. Make the youth leader's report a regular agenda item for the PCC (to add to support and accountability of the work). +Nt

8. Run a parish study day on youth work.+Nt

9. Encourage the whole Church to take an interest in youth work, for example by using it or issues that young people raise as the subject of a sermon. +Nt

10. Make sure that youth events are included in the general notices given out in church, in the magazine etc., so that they are seen as an integral part of the work of the Church. +Nt

11. Make available proper supervision formal and personal support to your youth workers (paid or unpaid). +Nt

12. Ensure that there is a careful selection of youth leaders (paid and unpaid), and involve young people in this. +Nt

13. Promote training for clergy and lay workers. Use the Spectrum Course and use local authority and other agencies' courses. Make sure that this training is appropriate, accessible and affordable. +Nt

Deanery

1. Arrange a deanery youth service/social event for joint support (termly?). +Gu

2. Appoint and support a youth worker coordinator to encourage working relationships between local ministry teams and within the archdeaconry. +Nt +Gu

3.   Affirm the youth workers outside the Church structures through formal introductions and informally, e.g. in schools, youth service. +Nt

4.   Add youth workers to prayer rotas. +Nt

Diocese

1.   Run a nationally recognised training programme for all youth workers. +KL

2.   Produce a diocesan newsletter to enhance communication. +Gu

3.   Arrange training days for youth workers. +Gu

4.   Arrange for youth workers to have contact with the bishop. +Gu

5.   Use networks that cross deanery boundaries to encourage support, shared resources. +Gu

6.   Twin with diocese from another part of the country to share ideas. +Gu

7.   Have an annual diocesan service. +Gu

8.   Arrange two or three well run 'good events' each year. +Gu

9.   Encourage and invite the senior staff of the church, 'the purple' to young people's events and study days. Encourage an interest in youth work by keeping these people informed and aware of what is happening in the diocese. +Nt

10. Establish a diocesan network of paid youth workers to ensure support and accountability. +Nt

11. Involve diocesan youth officers in the recruitment and employment of paid youth workers to help with good practice. +Nt

National

1.   Arrange recognition of training courses. +Gu

2.   Support the network of DYOs. +Gu

3.   Organise links with young people abroad. +Gu

4.   Support and encourage young people on General Synod. +Gu

**12.   We have a vision of a Church where clergy training has a signif-
icant emphasis on work with young people** (see paragraph 6.48 + 6.44-5).

Objectives from Consultations

Parish

1.   Encourage ongoing training for clergy and laity. Allocate a yearly
budget for training. +Gu

2.   Recognise the ability to delegate, support and encourage those
who are doing the youth work. +Gu

3.   Encourage the clergy to develop an understanding of youth work
and find ways for this work not to be marginalised in parish life.
+Gu +St

Deanery

1.   Establish support networks. +Gu

2.   Appoint a deanery clergy/laity youth co-ordinator. +Gu

Diocesan

1.   Ensure that all clergy attend a course on young people and youth
work on a 3-5 year basis. +Gu

2.   Ensure that diocesan budgets include appropriate funding for
youth work and training. +Gu

3.   Ensure that the diocesan youth officer and the staff are well
resourced. +Gu

National

1.   Input information about young people's needs and development to
the clergy training. +Gu

2.   Ensure adequate funding, resources and support of the National
Youth Office. +Gu

**13.   We have a vision of a Church which encourages partnerships
with other organisations which work with young people** (chapter 7).

Objectives from Consultations

General

1.   Value contacts with schools, higher education and further education colleges and find ways of improving these.

2. Value links with local education authorities and find ways of working to improve these.

3. Recognise the importance of full time personnel who are able to work with other agencies, e.g. diocesan youth officers.

4. Appreciate the importance of partnerships at a time when resources available are being reduced in many other sectors, for example look at sharing premises, staff, projects, etc.

5. Value, appreciate and work in partnership with uniformed organisations.

14. We have a vision of a Church which encourages partnerships with other denominations and Christian organisations which work with young people (see chapter 7).

Objectives from Consultations

General
1. Create a climate of honesty and respect for others' opinions (not necessarily agreement) and value and understand your own faith and work. +Nt

2. Be clear about the objectives and parameters of the partnership. Make sure that these are specific and that everyone is aware of the boundaries. +Nt

3. Use some of your resources to find out what other people or agencies are doing with young people.

4. Work co-operatively to assess needs of different groups and then agree how these needs may be met by working together or agreeing which are best tackled separately. +Nt

5. Areas for co-operation include:

Funding	Training	Resources
Celebrating	Research	Crime Prevention
Grieving	Advocacy	Developing our Faiths +Nt
Learning	Sharing Expertise	

15. We have a vision of a Church which sees youth work as one part of a faith journey which continues and develops as young people become older and their life circumstances change (see chapter 3).

Objectives from Consultations

General

1. Ensure that ordinands coming into parishes have done some youth work so that they are more attuned to young people. +SW +D

Parish

1. Encourage young people to build up an informal relationship with the vicar/youth leader. +SW +St

2. Use youth leaders to encourage others to listen to the ideas of young people and respect their point of view to 'bridge' gaps in understanding. +SW +Du

3. Follow up contacts with young people after confirmation, or any other links they may have with the Church.

4. Ensure that the atmosphere is not too formal or forbidding for young people, that there is a welcome and people are encouraged to keep in touch with each other. +SW

5. Give attention to the style of worship so that young people can 'connect' with this. +Du

16. We have a vision of a Church which appreciates that young people have their own ways of expressing themselves and distinct cultures which they will bring to the Church (see chapter 1).

Objectives from Consultations

General

1. Have 'quotas' in place in all committees within the Church to ensure young people's participation. +Gu +SW

2. See variety and the huge range of youth work in the Church as positive. +Gu

3. Highlight the importance of effective communication. +Gu

4. Listen to young people – do not assume what they want. Provide a focus for them so that their ideas can be made known. +KL +SW

5. Arrange training or events which help adults to develop sensitivity to young people. +SW

6. Ensure the work is properly resourced. +SW

7. Spread the word that the work of including young people needs effort from everybody, and value young people as an integral part of the Church. +SW

Parish

1. Ensure equal participation in worship, readings, prayers and Church structures, e.g. PCCs. +Gu +SW

2. Create a culture where young people work alongside older people in the life of the Church. +Ke

3. Establish young people's groups which can send representatives to lobby adult groups. +Ke

4. Provide opportunities for young people to celebrate either with other young people or in all-age worship. +Ke +SW

5. Help remove the fear within existing congregations that by giving young people time and space they will lose everything that is important to them. +KL

Deanery

1. Appoint youth workers at deanery level.+Gu

National

1. Relax Canon Law concerning liturgy. +Gu

2. Work to build a national young person network. +Gu

3. Produce a national quarterly Church of England youth magazine. +Gu

4. Make opportunities or produce literature for people to understand/experience young people's culture. +Ke

Appendix

Types of Youth Work

A large number of dioceses and parishes responded to the request for information as to what youth work was happening in their area. Below is a list of the wide range of youth work currently taking place throughout the country (see paragraph 7.2).

Parish-based

Continuation of Sunday School – meeting during service/Sunday evening
 – class system (11-13 etc) / peer group moves up together
'House-group' model – discussion participation (e.g. small group of young people meet each week for study and fellowship)
Fun with a 'God slot' – weekday evening, social, with outgoings
Choir-based – peer support and social life
Servers
Bellringers
Worship/music/drama/dance group
Confirmation groups – pre-confirmation/post-confirmation
Marriage preparation and counselling
Baptism preparation for parents and godparents
Bereavement counselling
Basics/nurture group
Residential weekends
Rural/suburban/inner city characteristics
Parish-based youth workers
Part-time/full-time
Qualified/unqualified
Paid/accommodation and pocket money/unpaid

Area/deanery-based

Rural youth projects (e.g. projects funded by rural development commission, trusts, parishes, etc.)
Deanery youth festival
Deanery youth service
Cross-parish youth clubs
Deanery post-confirmation days
Area-based mobile work (e.g. bus/caravan projects)

Diocesan

Diocesan Youth Action Team (e.g. young adults committed to helping their parishes in their work with early adolescents)
Diocese Challenger Scheme (e.g. young people undertake projects with local older partners)

Diocesan post-confirmation weekend
Diocesan youth officer run events
Diocesan festivals

Education-based

School chaplaincies
Church of England secondary schools
Scripture Union schools' worker
Further education/university chaplaincies
Student Christian Movement
Church of England groups e.g. Anglican Society
Theological colleges
School visits and work, e.g. producing information book for years 10–12, assemblies and
    Christian Unions
Universities and Colleges Christian Fellowship
Ecumenical
Ecumenical co-operation, e.g. joint events/activities
Council of Churches

Not in-house

Open youth work
Mixed open/in-house youth work (e.g. work on council housing estate with 14+ drawing young
    people into the Church)
'Albermarle Report' youth centres (parishes involved in running youth centres built in partner-
    ship with the DES in the 1960s)
Detached youth work projects, e.g. Oxford Youth Works
Church Urban Fund (the CUF report of 1993 details projects in various dioceses)
Detached youth work
Projects supported by DFEE grant

Worship-based

Parish youth service – special
Youth services based in deanery or area
Taizé music
Large (alternative) worship events
Grapevine worship events
Alternative worship work in parishes

Training

Spectrum
Volunteer Schemes
Diocesan Youth Leader Training

Larger events/externally organised work

Pathfinders, CYFA Ventures, camps
SU beach missions

Diocesan/deanery events
- concerts
- all-night events, sleep-outs
- residential – house parties/camps

Evangelistic events/rallies

Events based around interest groups (e.g. theatre workshops)
Sport/specific issues, e.g. sexism
Input from diocesan officers/groups in other ministries e.g. FLAME, vocations and ordination training
Anglican Youth rallies
Youth pilgrimages, e.g. Iona, Archbishop to Taizé
Youth houses/residential centres

Organisations involved with young people

Scripture Union
Church Missionary Society
CARE (Christian Initiative on Teenage Sexuality)
Anglican Youth
Christian Youth Contact Service
YMCA, YWCA
Youth for Christ
Committee on Black Anglican Concerns
Church Army
Girls' Friendly Society
Boys' Brigade
Girls' Brigade
Church Lads'/Girls' Brigade
Church Youth Fellowship Association (CPAS)
Scouts, Guides, Ventures, Rangers – Anglican Fellowship of Scouts and Guides
Children's Society
Frontier Youth Trust
Crusaders

Young adults

Young adult forums
Young adults' groups, e.g. 17+ group
Youth participation

Bibliography

William Abrahams, *The Logic of Evangelism*, Hodder and Stoughton, 1989.

Advisory Board of Ministry, *Opportunities for Service, Overseas and at Home*, 1994.

Nick Aitken, ed., *Creative Ideas for Youth Evangelism*, Marshall Pickering, 1992.

Gillian Ambrose, Andrew Gear and David Green, *The Discovery Wheel*, National Society/Church House Publishing, 1994.

Brian Appleyard, *Understanding the Present*, Picador, 1993.

Mark Ashton, *Christian Youthwork*, Kingsway, 1986.

Jett Astley, 'Faith development and young people', unpublished paper, 1995.

Andy Back, *101 Dynamic Ideas for your Youth Group*, Word UK Ltd, 1991.

Zygmunt Bauman, *Deceiving the 20th century*, New Statesman and Society, 1st April 1994.

David Bosch, *Witness to the World: The Christian Mission in Theological Perspective*, Marshall, Morgan & Scott, 1980.

Breaking New Ground: Church Planting in the Church of England, Church House Publishing, 1994.

Mike Breen, *Outside In*, Scripture Union, 1993.

George Carey, *Spiritual Journey*, Mowbrays, 1994.

Francis Cattermole, Audenshaw paper, no. 131, December 1990.

Steve Chalke, *The Complete Youth Manual*, vol. 1, Kingsway, 1987.

Children's Society, *The Way it is*, 1994.

Tim Clapton, 'The religious experience and faith development of non-churchgoing young people', unpublished MTh, Westminster College, Oxford, 1993.

Graham Cray, *From Here to Where? The Culture of the 90s*, Board of Mission Occasional Paper No. 3.

Graham Cray, *The Gospel and Tomorrow's Culture: Learning to Communicate the Gospel in Today's World*, CPAS, 1994.

Terry Dunnell, *Mission and Young People at Risk*, Frontier Youth Trust, 1995.

Erik Erikson, *Young Man Luther*, Norton, 1958.

John Finney, *Finding Faith Today: How does it Happen?*, Bible Society, 1992.

James Fowler, *Becoming Adult, Becoming Christian*, Harper and Row, 1984.

James Fowler, *Stages of Faith: the Psychology of Human Development and the Quest for Meaning*, Harper and Row, 1981.

Leslie Francis (ed.), *Fast Moving Currents in Youth Culture*, Lynx, 1995.

Leslie Francis, *Making Contact*, Collins, 1986.

Leslie Francis and David Lankshear, 'Changing trends in Anglican confirmation', *Journal of Empirical Theology*, vol.6 no.1, 1993, pp 64-76.

Robin Gill, *Moral Communities*, University of Exeter Press, 1992.

Good News in our Times: the Gospel and Contemporary Cultures, Church House Publishing, 1991.

Charles Handy, *The Age of Unreason*, Arrow, 1995.

Stanley Hauerwas and William H. Willimon, *Resident Alien*, Abingdon, 1989.

Simon Heathfield, *Rave On*, CPAS, 1994.

Robert Hewison, *Future Tense: A New Art for the Nineties*, Methuen, 1990.

Paul Hooper, *Being Young in an Old Church*, Grove, 1986.

Charles Jencks, *What is Post-modernism?*, Academy Editions, 1986.

Stephen Jones, *Faith Shaping*, Judson Press, 1987.

John Lee, *Spiritual Development*, Diocese of Bath and Wells, 1991.

Clifford Longley, Introduction to Jonathan Sacks, *Faith in the Future*, Darton, Longman and Todd, 1995.

D. Lyon, *Postmodernity*, Open University Press, 1994.

Mark McCann, *Relational Youth Ministry, a Core Team Model*, St Mary's Press, 1995.

Nick Mercer, 'Postmodernity and rationality: The final credits or just a commercial break?' in Billington, Lane and Turner (eds) *Mission and Meaning: Essays Presented to Peter Cotterell*, Paternoster, 1995.

John Millbank, *Theology and Social Theory*, Blackwell, 1990.

A Time for Sharing: Collaborative Ministry in Mission, Board of Mission Occasional Paper No. 6, and GS Misc 465, 1995.

Mission in Action, Bible-based Resources for Youth Groups. Ten sessions on mission for 13 – 18 year olds, CPAS, 1995.

Bob Moffat, *Crowdbreakers*, Marshall Pickering, 1992.

Jurgen Moltman, *The Open Church*, SCM, 1978.

Hugh Montefiore (ed.), *The Gospel and Contemporary Culture*, Mowbray, 1992.

Phil Moon, *Young People and the Bible*, Marshall Pickering, 1992.

Lesslie Newbigin, *The Gospel in a Pluralist Society*, SPCK, 1989.

Lesslie Newbigin, *The Other Side of 1984*, WCC (Risk), 1984.

Lance Pierson, *The Pastoral Care of Young People*, Grove, 1985.

Edward Robinson and Michael Jackson, *Religion and Values at Sixteen Plus*, Alistair Hardy Research Centre/Christian Education Movement, 1987.

Jonathan Sacks, *The Persistence of Faith*, Weidenfeld and Nicholson, 1991.

Mike Starkey, *Fashion and Style*, Monarch, 1995.

Peter Stow, *Youth in the City*, Hodder and Stoughton, 1987.

Charles Taylor, *Sources of the Self*, Cambridge University Press, 1989.

Alvin Toffler, *Future Shock*, Pan, 1973.

Tomorrow is Another Country: Education in a Post-modern World, Church House Publishing, 1996.

James Torrance, 'The Forgotten Trinity'. Report of the BCC study commission on Trinitarian doctrine today, Costa Carras and James Thomas (eds), British Council of Churches, 1989-91.

Denis Tully, 'The Church, young people and adults', unpublished paper, 1995.

David Tyndall, 'Journeying and dwelling', unpublished paper, 1995.

Gianni Vattimo, trans. Jon R. Snyder, *The End of Modernity*, Polity Press, 1988.

Jim Wallis, *Agenda for Biblical People*, Triangle, 1986.

Pete Ward, *Youth Culture and the Gospel*, Marshall Pickering, 1992.

Ward, Adam and Levermore, *Youth Work and How to Do it*, Lynx, 1994.

Robert Warren, *Being Human, Being Church*, Harper Collins, 1995.

Robert Warren, *Building Missionary Congregations: Towards a Post-modern Way of being Church*, Church House Publishing, 1995 (Board of Mission Occasional Paper No.4 and GS Misc 446).

Pip Wilson, *Games Without Frontiers*, Marshall Pickering, 1988.

Nicholas Thomas Wright, *The New Testament and the People of God*, SPCK, 1982.

Index

abuse 8
accessibility 1–17
accountability
    in worship 67, 69
    in youth work 125, 166, 167
adolescence 27–8
Albermarle Report 149
alcohol 8
alternative worship 68–69, 82
Anglican Youth 75, 83–4, 154–5
Appleyard, B. 29
Astley, J. 44, 61
attendance at Church 12–13

Ball, P. 18, 20
baptism 94
Bauman, Zygmunt 11
Bell, J. 50
Be Real 68
Bernard, Brother, SSF 23
Bilsthorpe Community Project 21
Black Anglican Youth 9
Borgmann, Dean 2
Bosch, D. 23
Boys' Brigade 141
BPM 68
Breaking New Ground 67
Brice, P. 58, 59
Bruno, S. 9, 76
Bryant, Mark 138–39
bullying 7

Careforce 78
Carey, George, Archbishop 36
Cattermole, F. 40
Centre Light Trust 18–19
Challenger Scheme (Truro) 97
challenges 10–11
Champion House (Derby) 51–52, 98
Chelmsford Youth Worker Training 82
Children Act (1989) 103, 110, 124, 166
Children's Society 7, 9
Children's Special Service Mission (CSSM) 154
Christians in Sport 81
church attendance 12–13
Church Girls' Brigade 115–16, 141
Church Lads' Brigade 115–16, 141
Church of England Young People's Assembly (CEYPA) 155–57
Church of England Youth Council (CEYC) 151–3
Church of England Youth Services (CEYS) 127

Churches Outreach Project (Leicester) 18–19
Church Missionary Society (CMS) 48
Church Pastoral Aid Society (CPAS) 47, 76
Church Urban Fund 20–21
Church Youth Fellowship Association 47, 154
Clapton, T. 40–1
clergy
    involvement 125–6
    training 120, 126, 167
community 83
community-based work 21–2
confirmation 94–98
consultation 163, 165
    Church structures 72–5, 84, 168
    on worship 71–2
Cooking Something Different 68
Cooper, R. 80–1
Crathorne Campsite (York) 52
Cray, Graham 2
cross of Christ 35–6
Crusaders 52, 144
culture
    contributions to 30–32
    formation 28–30

development of faith
    stages 42–4
    within the Church 45–54
diocesan networks 127–29
diocesan synods 73
diocesan youth officers 101, 108, 119, 156–7, 166
    networks 127–9, 136
Diocesan Youth Officers' Conference (1995) 45
discipleship 36–8
discrimination 8–9, 165
drugs 8
Dyer, C. 92

ecumenical work 129, 145–6
education 55–59, 158, 159
    changes in 58–59, 158–59
    further 57–58
    higher 58–59
    schools 55–57
Edward King Institute 160
Ellis, J. 98
Elms, R. 28
Emmanuel Youth Project (East London) 77
employees 109–17
Enlightenment 29
environment 32, 41, 165

Erikson, Eric 44
European Values Study 29
Evaluation 117–18
evangelism 6

Falcon Holidays 47
faith
    development 42–3
    journey 168
    nurturing 85–6
family problems 8, 164
Far Forest Centre (Worcester) 56
Finney, J. 43
Fogwill, O. 144
Foreman, A. 27, 84
Fowler, J. 42–3
Foxton Centre (Blackburn) 21
Francis, L. and Lankshear, D. 13–14, 65, 75, 94–97,
    100, 125, 141–2
Frontier Youth Trust 76, 128
funding 10, 158, 162

Gap, The (Swindon) 90
General Synod 73
General Synod Youth Affairs Group 157
Giddens, A. 33
Gill, R. 31
Girls' Brigade 141
Girls' Friendly Society 47, 142
gospel
    as story 34–5
    need for 36–7
Green, D. 100
Greenbelt 48–49, 68, 155
Guides Association 139–140

Handy, C. 27
Hauerwas, S. 38
health and safety 123–4
Hiebert, G. 14
Hill, M. 14–15
Hit Squad 46
Holiday Bible Clubs 19
holidays 52
homelessness 7, 164

identity, personal and social 33–4
Incarnation 25, 35
insurance 124–5
interfaith work 146–47

Jackson, M. 44
James, W. 10
Jenkins, C. 57
Jenkins, T. 56
John Francis, Brother 40

Lankshear, D. 57, 59
    see also Francis and Lankshear
Late Service, The 68
leaders, young people as 75, 164
Lee, J. 60–1
Local Education Authorities 130–36
Local Council of Voluntary Youth Services (LCVYS)
    127–28
Longley, Clifford 49
Loweswater Youth Festival (Cumbria) 49
Lyon, D. 26

marriage 94
Mercer, N. 11, 12
Millbank, J. 34
Milson-Fairbairn Report 150
mission of Church
    context 25–6
    integration 24
    nature of 23
    tasks 23–4
mission of young people 162–3, 169
model
    Jesus Christ as 58
models of work 15–16
Moon, P. 69
Morning Star Trust 53
Mothers' Union 48
Music and Worship Workshops (York) 49

National Society 7, 58, 59
National Youth Agency 57
National Youth Office 66, 73, 129–30
Nine O'Clock Service 69

Oasis 121
objectives 169–187
On the Edge Project (Truro) 145
outreach work 86–91, 162, 163
overseas exchanges 52
Oxford Youth Works 91, 121

parents 85
parish-based work 91–3
Parochial Church Councils 71, 72–3, 163
partnership 168
Pathfinders 46, 47, 154
peer groups 82–3, 84–5
personal development 32–5, 61–2
pilgrimages 54
Platform For Young Women 47
Popham, D. 19
post-modernism 11
principles of youth work 17–18

quality of youth work 121–26, 165–66

racism 9
Rank Foundation 116
Rave in the Nave 70
recommendations 162–9
recruitment 111–15
Redcliffe-Maud, Lord 149
relationship with God 36
residentials 50–52, 155
    Chelmsford Diocese 50
Resurrection 35
resourcing parish work 92–3
resources 118–20, 162
retreats 53
Richards, A. 2
Richards, G. 101
Richardson, John 6, 14, 15–16
Roberts, P. 68, 69
Robinson, E. 44
Royal School of Church Music 66
rural areas 18–20
Rural Contact Project 87

Sacks, J. 27
'Safe from Harm' 103, 110, 124, 166
St Andrew's Youth Club (Halifax) 121–2
St Chad's (Coventry) 89–90
St Chad's Community Project (Gateshead) 77
St John's Church (Woodbridge) 109–10, 113–14
St John's Youth Project (Southall) 87
St Peter's (Bengeworth) 105
St Thomas' Project (Birmingham) 21
Schulze 28
Scouts Association 138–40
Scripture Union 48
sexuality 8
Shalom Project (Grimsby) 88–9, 107
Shelter 7
Snyder, J.R. 26
social justice 41
Soul Survivor (Watford) 90
Spectrum 106–7, 120, 146
spiritual guidance 60–1
spirituality 39–62, 64, 164
    and religion 40
    and religious experience 40–1
Spring Harvest 155
student debt 58
support 113–15, 165, 166
    for volunteers 107–9

Taizé 54–5
Taylor, C. 30
Taylor, Herbert, Canon 154
Thompson Report 150
Time for God 78, 129–30
Toffler, A. 11
Torrance, J. 30
training 115–17, 151, 163, 166, 167
    volunteers 105–7
Tully, D. 16, 72
Turnbull Commission 160
Tyndall, D. 42

unemployment 7,
uniformed organisations 76, 82, 138–42
urban areas 20–21, 86–7
Urwin, Lindsay, Bishop 65, 74
USPG (United Society for the Propagation of the
    Gospel) 48

Venner, Stephen, Bishop 81
volunteers 89–90, 104–9

Wallis, J. 25
Walsingham 53
Warren, R. 66, 79, 83
Water 4 Life 77–8
Wild Hope 68
Willimon, W.H. 38
worship 45–6, 63–72, 164, 169
    alternative 68–9
    experimentation 70–1
    roles in 64–6
Wright, N.T. 33

YMCA 116, 142–4
youth congregations 66–7
Youth for Christ 48
Youth Service Development Council 18
Youth Sunday 66
Youth Synod 73–4
Youth Training 7
youth workers 100–26
    employment 109–18
    volunteers 104–9
YWCA 116–7, 142–4

Zone, The (Nottingham) 89–90